The DALAI LAMA'S
BIG BOOK *of* HAPPINESS

The DALAI LAMA'S
BIG BOOK *of* HAPPINESS

How to Live in Freedom, Compassison, and Love

HIS HOLINESS THE DALAI LAMA
EDITED BY RENUKA SINGH

Cover design by Jim Warner
Cover art by © Eddie Adams / Corbis
Interior designed by Kathryn Sky-Peck

Hampton Roads Publishing Company, Inc.
Charlottesville, VA 22906
Distributed by Red Wheel/Weiser, LLC
www.redwheelweiser.com

Sign up for our newsletter and special offers by going to
www.redwheelweiser.com/newsletter/.

ISBN: 978-1-57174-739-6

Library of Congress Cataloging-in-Publication Data available upon request

Printed in Canada

FR

10 9 8 7 6 5 4 3 2 1

Editor's Dedication

To
The Long Life of His Holiness
The Dalai Lama till Samsara Ends

CONTENTS

Foreword

BUDDHISM HAS DIRECTED THE path of His Holiness the Dalai Lama's development—both inner and outer—and remains a guide for humanity's course of becoming. The lectures compiled in this collection do not deal directly with the goal of enlightenment or Buddhahood. Rather, they highlight universal themes of compassion; non-violence and peace; secular ethics; a healthy body, mind, individual, and society; and the human potential for happiness through one's inner realizations. People the world over appear ready to receive the wisdom emanating from and about Buddhism that directly protects us from our sufferings.

As mentioned in the lectures, we all have the capacity to get rid of intellectual conceptions and negative emotions in order to avoid experiencing worldly turbulence and suffering in our lives. However, this does not imply that we cannot or should not try to reach full Enlightenment, self-liberation from samsaric sufferings or, at least, to achieve a peaceful state of mind.

These lectures also symbolize the spiritual deprivation of people from all parts of the world, as is evident in the scope of invitations His Holiness receives from various countries, universities, and organizations. Moreover, His Holiness often reiterates that human beings, irrespective of whether they are atheists or believers, remain at the core of human deliverance with their unique historical potential.

At any given moment, human beings can either elevate themselves to the state of liberation or descend into the quagmire of demoniac existence. The responsibility to transform body, speech, and mind in various cultural settings ultimately lies with individuals. In other words, thoughts and actions acquire a kind of non-contradictoriness and transport one to become truly humane.

The lectures herein reveal not only how human beings act but how, through their daily effort and perseverance, they can claim their uniqueness to conduct themselves in a wholesome manner, befitting their inherent nature, and become the awakened one, to preserve humanity. It is high time that humanity expels utopian designs and learns to face facts by strengthening individual integrity. One is obliged, therefore, to live humanely, which will, perhaps, become the root of equality. Also, if we do not cultivate compassion and inner peace, even world peace won't bring us our inner equilibrium.

Let us conclude with the example of Richard More from Ireland who works very closely with His Holiness in improving the lives of others. More's work with children in crossfire or conflict situations and his remarkable life story is indeed inspirational. He lost his eyesight in 1972 after being shot by a rubber bullet. Richard had the magnanimity to invite and extend a warm welcome to the soldier who blinded him to His Holiness's talk at the University of Limerick in 2011. His Holiness's message of compassion and forgiveness resonated very deeply in Richard's act of not harboring any anger or bitterness toward Charles, the soldier responsible for his condition. Incidentally, both Richard and Charles have built up deep friendships with His Holiness now.

Similarly, through these lectures, followed by questions and answers, many people will be able to relate to His Holiness and his insightful wisdom with greater ease.

Renuka Singh

2013

Acknowledgments

MY DEEPEST GRATITUDE TO His Holiness the Dalai Lama, my root guru, for permitting me to work on his speeches given on various occasions at different places in the world. His Holiness's magnanimity of spirit is awe-inspiring. Thanks are also due to the Office of His Holiness, his secretaries, Chime Rigzin and Tenzin Taklha, for all their help in procuring the lectures for this book.

Special thanks are due to Ven. Ailsa Cameron, Kamalini Mukherjee, and Geshe Dorji Damdul for all their invaluable help in the preparation of this manuscript.

Chiki Sarkar, Shahnaz Siganporia, Chinmayee Manjunath, Niyati Dhuldhoya, and Monidipa Mondal at Penguin helped in facilitating the production of this book. Thanks. We have tried our very best to edit His Holiness's speeches minimally, so that the original flavor of his expression can be retained.

Finally, I wish to express my appreciation to my family—the Pauls in the United States—for supporting all my endeavors, spiritual and worldly. I hope my two grand-nephews, Sam and Harry, will one day go through this collection.

Editor's Note

"I ALWAYS SPEAK IN an informal way as it complements my broken English," says His Holiness in one of the speeches in this volume. To keep alive his voice and its particular flavor, we have left the speeches largely unchanged.

Renuka Singh
2013

Part One

THE SECRET
OF HAPPINESS

1

THE ART OF HAPPINESS

New Delhi, 2011

Getting older, sometimes my eyes give me some problems, so very strong light is not good. And usually I give my talks without notes, so light is not necessary. So dear brothers and sisters, indeed I am very happy having this opportunity to talk, or rather lecture, for Penguin. You organized this opportunity; thank you very much. When I give a talk to people, I always have the feeling we are the same human being—mentally, emotionally, physically. And more importantly, everyone wants a happy life. I think nobody, early in the morning, as soon as they wake up, wishes for more trouble in the day. Nobody wants trouble. However, many troubles are essentially our own creation. Why? Here is the big contradiction.

I think because of two things—the first is a lack of knowing the reality, which also is due to the lack of a holistic view. That's one thing. The other thing is too much self-centered attitude. These two things—the lack of knowledge about the reality and a self-centered attitude—are, I think, what creates unnecessary problems. We can't say this problem happened because of this or because of that. We have to realize that the ultimate factor of these problems is within ourselves.

So now, how to remove that? Not through prayer, not through money, not through power, but through understanding and awareness. We may say wisdom. So, now, happiness; every-body, including animals, wants less disturbances, less problems. So also we human beings, of course. Before talking about the source of happiness, I think it is maybe useful to know something about the systems of our minds. Because pleasure and happiness are part of our minds; and sadness, painful experience—these are also part of our minds.

Usually, you see, people simply have the sort of feeling or impression that the mind is one thing, one entity, something independent, something absolute. Up to now, as a result of my meeting many scientists on many occasions, I have realized that in the scientific field, they are still not clear so much about distinction between sensorial mind and the basic mind—mental consciousness. So it is important to make that distinction. You have the consciousness of the mind and mental consciousness.

Now usually, you see people seeking some sort of pleasure or some happy sort of experiences, but they mainly rely on the sensorial level. Look at some beautiful things—eye consciousness; beautiful music—ear consciousness. Similarly taste, smell, even sex. So these are five kinds of positive experiences, mainly on a sensorial level, but they are a very temporary sort of experience. As long as the music is there, you feel happy; but then it stops. And seeing something beautiful, you feel happy; once that is gone—no. So the happiness felt at a sensorial level is short-lived.

Now to the mental level. If we develop a certain positive experience on the mental level, that remains long-lasting. Then also, some experiences are a calmer, peaceful, pleasant sort of feeling. At the sensorial level, even if something is sort of disturbing—a voice, a noise, or a difficult facility, poor facility or physical illness—this sort of pain can be subdued with a more mental-level calmness. On the other hand, if the mental level contains too much fear, too much anxiety, too much stress, no experience that the sensorial level enjoys can subdue that mental-level anxiety or fear. So, obviously, mental-level experiences are more important than sensorial-level experiences. I think, if we pay some attention, everybody would realize this.

We say that at the mental level, happiness is not necessarily a feeling of pleasure. I think happiness here, mainly, is in the sense of satisfaction. Even though physical-level suffering is a painful experience, it may bring deep satisfaction at the mental level. So happiness mainly refers to the consciousness level—the mental level. Now, of course, all major religious traditions are trying to bring calm, peace or a positive sort of feeling in the mental level.

In most cases, I think there is a common factor to all religious traditions—theistic religion, non-theistic religion or one sort of practice—is that of faith. So faith is not a thing of the sensorial level; faith is the sixth consciousness or mental-level consciousness. Of course, the sensorial consciousness helps in listening to some music, some praying and things like that, or looking at an image of the Buddha, an image of God, an image of Jesus Christ or an image of Shivji. Of course it helps, but the real sort of effect must work on mental consciousness. Faith does not take place on a sensorial level, but in mental consciousness. And then the practice of love, compassion, and with that, forgiveness, tolerance, contentment—all these belong to the sixth mental level, the mental-level consciousness.

Then non-theistic religious tradition—such as one part of Sankhya—is a very old Indian tradition, I think almost 3,000 years old, or more than 3,000 years. Then, at the time of Buddha, Jainism and Buddhism—these two new non-theistic religions—developed. These non-theistic religious traditions have no idea of a creator but believe in the law of causality—cause and effect.

Everybody knows in this country about the law of karma. Karma means action—whether it is physical action, verbal action, or mental action. If you look at the world with a positive eye or a sincere motivation like compassion or forgiveness, then certain sort of emotion comes; that's karma. It is positive or good karma, because its motivation is something good—a sense of concern for others' well-being, which is a benefit to others and a benefit to oneself and therefore considered positive. There is no absolute positive or negative. Likewise anger, hatred, suspicion may be of two kinds—positive and negative. But, in a way, some negative sort of motivation ultimately brings discomfort to oneself or another; it causes negative karma.

These two are different approaches, but the aim is the same—strengthening love, compassion, forgiveness, and so forth. A theistic religion uses the concept of God, a creator; a non-theistic one uses the concept of law of causality—if you do good things to another, you get benefit; if you do harm to another, you get a negative result, consequences like that. But then, even without relating with religious faith, there is another way. Religions are all related with some mysterious things. But without touching any mysterious thing, on the basis of obvious things, we can show, or we can educate people that warm-heartedness or an affectionate or compassionate heart is the source of happiness.

Firstly, biologically, among all social animals, including some birds, there is some kind of responsibility for their group. The reality is that the individual's survival, happiness, and well-being depend on the rest of the group. Because of that reality, a sense of some kind of community and unity concerns the rest of the group. We belong to that group; so no matter what, one single powerful person cannot survive alone. Not only a happy life but survival itself depends on the rest of the community. That's a fact. Because of that, there must be some emotion that brings people together, and that's affection toward each other. Anger expels. So affection and compassion are a part of our mind for survival.

Now here, at this level, other animals are the same—dogs, cats, many birds have this same sort of ability, sort of nature. We human beings have this marvellous human intelligence so that on the basis of it, for long-term interest and a wider perspective, we can increase . . . compassion, which is biologically developed. Here, the compassion or love is mainly on a biological sort of level; it is limited, biased, and also often goes with hatred or suspicion. After that, there is the second level of compassion—love through training, with the use of human intelligence, the use of reason, logic, or in the interest of the wider or long-term perspective, that can actually become unbiased.

Let me give one clear example. The biological factor of love or compassion can develop toward your friend; toward your enemy, you develop compassion instead of hatred, anger, suspicion. Because the biological level is very much oriented toward others' attitude, your friend's attitude is good for you, so you love them. Your enemy's attitude is harmful for you, therefore you respond toward them with anger, negative things. Now use human intelligence—irrespective of whether the individual is a friend or enemy or neutral, he or she is still part of the community. Your life depends on the community. Members of the community are not all necessarily your friends; some disagreeable people are also part of the community. Now in today's world, even if two people have a sort of negative attitude toward each other, for survival they both need each other.

So I often see the expression in today's world of all sorts of century-old strong feelings—we and they, and between the two some kind of solid wall. We don't care for others, and even wish some bad things for them. That is an old way of thinking. In ancient times, each community, each nation was more or less independent. Now, today, everything is dependent on others. According to that reality, that strong concept of "we and they" is now outdated. We must consider the rest of the humanity; the rest of the world is part of "we," because our interests depend on them.

Therefore, using these sorts of reasons, we can extend our genuine sense of concern and well-being not on the basis of people's attitude, but on the basis that they are one of our community. Irrespective of the individual's attitude toward you, both of you are still part of the community. We can extend our love, compassion toward the others on that level. That animals cannot do. We human beings, using our intelligence, can. We have developed the potential for a level of compassion that is unbiased; it is genuine compassion.

Here, it is important to make a distinction. If your so-called enemy creates problems for you, as far as the action is concerned, you may take appropriate countermeasure. But as a human being, you still can keep compassion and a sense of concern for their well-being. In fact, if you let their wrongdoing continue without check, ultimately they will suffer. So out of sense of concern of their long-term well-being, take countermeasure to stop their wrongdoing. So that kind of attitude looks like countermeasure, but is actually a sort of good work. These are the sort of ways of training our mind—not through meditation but through utilizing our intelligence, through analyzing. Through that way, our concept, you see, can change.

Once you develop your mental attitude, make it more realistic—based on reason—and more open, then you can maintain happiness. Happiness here has very much to do with a calm mind. No stress, no anxiety, no fear. On one level, you can see negative things, but at a deeper level you can still keep a calm mind, irrespective of whether you are a religious believer or non-believer. Nowadays in scientific findings, often you will see they say, "Healthy body, healthy mind'—there is a very close link. An agitated mind for a longer period is really very, very harmful for our physical health. A calm mind is a healthy mind; no matter the circumstances, if you can keep a healthy mind, then that brings immense benefit to your physical health.

Actually some scientists, in our meetings on many occasions, tell me, "Fear, anger, hatred are actually eating away our immune systems." On the other hand, keep your mind calm, take less stress, and it is very helpful to your immune system. On one occasion in New York, one medical scientist mentioned to me that according to his findings, those people who often express in "I, me, mine" have a greater risk of having a heart attack. The reason, of course, is that such people cherish themselves very much and are too much self-centered, so with that kind of attitude even small problems appear unbearable.

Once you develop a more open heart, more sense of concern for others' well-being, I say the inner door opens. Firstly, through that way, you can communicate with other people very easily. That brings you more friends, which reduces the feeling of loneliness and increases compassionate attitude, which immensely helps to reduce anxiety, stress. So it is very useful for our health. After all, as I had mentioned earlier, man is a social animal, so these mental attitudes go well with our reality.

I think, generally, people stress the importance of education. Very right. Many problems arise due to the lack of knowledge, due to ignorance. So through education, we are equipped to look at the world in a wider, comprehensive way, so that we get the holistic picture. Actually, the very purpose of education is to reduce the gap between appearance and reality. So education should be more holistic—that is, I think, very important. Then, on the basis of scientific finding, positive emotions are very important for our health, and a happy individual means a happy family and a happy community.

Now, I think I am seventy-six. At sixteen I lost my freedom; at twenty-four I became a refugee—stateless and homeless. In a way, I lost a small home—Tibet—but I found a big home—India. So in any way, my life went through turbulence but I think, comparatively, my mind is quite peaceful. I hope the peace is not due to dullness. I think my mind is quite sharp. When I engage with really famous scientists, when they talk, my knowledge compared with them of course is almost zero. But we are trained in the Nalanda sort of tradition—every single point we analyze, logically analyze. That really helps immensely to sharpen our minds. So I hope my mind is not that dull.

However, you see that despite turbulent experiences in life, my mind is comparatively quite calm. The immediate result is that my health is very good. Actually, you see, that important organ, my gallbladder is gone, about I think two or three years ago through surgery. This body looks like a very normal human being, but one important human organ is missing. (*Laughs*) But basically, my health is very good. I think my mental state really makes all the difference—this I feel. Some physicians, after they check my physical condition, often say that it is not like that of a person over seventy, but looks ten years younger.

So some people describe me as a reincarnation of Avalokiteshvara. I don't know whether I am a truly reincarnated higher being or not. I know my own mind; I can read my own mind. But I think even a human being who utilizes his human intelligence properly results in being mentally happy, physically healthy. Isn't it? Everybody has this same sort of potential. Whether they pay sufficient attention to it or not, or sufficient awareness or not—that is the point. Otherwise they all have the same potential. That's what my talk is about—the art of happiness. Clear?

So now, some of the ancient Indian treasures are a detailed knowledge about human emotions, about the human mind.

Irrespective of whether you look at Buddhism, Jainism, or Hinduism, they all have some common practices—the practice of Samatha, the practice of Vipassana are both a certain sort of mental training. Naturally, a lot of explanation about the mind—something like a map of emotions, a map of mind—I think that will really need more study to discover. The world of the mind is so vast that it is very important to know the system—different minds, how they develop, how they work. That is important. The same way, you see, when you are taking medical care of the physically ill, you should know the physical system and how it works.

On the mental level also, we should know the whole system of the mind—the mental world as an academic subject, not a religious subject. When that knowledge is used for concepts like the next life, or heaven or even hell, then it is related with religion. But simply the well-being of this world, of this life, has nothing to do with religion; we can separate this sort of information used for a religious way from that used for a secular way.

So I often tease my Indian friends. You see, they every day worship one of their gods, goddesses, some flower, some incense; and repeat some sentences of Sanskrit shlokas, Sanskrit verses, but without knowing their meaning—there is not much use in this. We must pay more attention, study the richness of Indian philosophy and Indian thought. That is very important.

I often express that religious faith and injustice of action, like corruption, cannot go together. There is no third choice; only two: a faithful, religious-minded, caring, honest, truthful life of justice; or a corrupt life, denying God, denying karma, just seeking money and power. It is a really big contradiction when you pray to Shivji, pray to Ganesh, but meantime have no hesitation about corruption. This is a big contradiction.

Whether you are a believer or a nonbeliever, if the whole society is more clean and transparent, everybody feels happy. The nation can be built more rapidly. If there is a lot of corruption, a lot of injustice, then millions of poor people suffer the most. India is still the most populated democratic nation. Over the last sixty years, India, I think, has been a very stable country because of democracy, rule of law. So the people of India should think that at this level—how to build a healthy India. Each Indian individual has the moral responsibility to build India in a more healthy way. Then India can truly make a significant impact on the world, because of its the size, because of long history. Thank you.

QUESTIONS

QUESTION: *I would really appreciate for you to talk about difference between self-centeredness and self-love. Self-love is quite often misunderstood and abused as self-centeredness, but it is essential to being compassionate. And it would be wonderful to hear your view.*

HIS HOLINESS: So, the love or sense of concern of well-being. Unless you care for yourself or love your self, you cannot extend love to others. First, love and cherish yourself, and then consider that an infinite number of sentient beings also—just like you— want a happy life, do not want suffering. Since you really take care of yourself, in a similar sort of condition you must extend your sense of concern of well-being to the infinite sentient beings. A self-centered attitude is to not care about others, just think of one's self and for one's own interest—to not only neglect others' well-being, but even bully, take advantage, exploit—these things.

Here, a self-centered attitude and also what you call the strong sense of self, is very necessary in order to develop determination, willpower. For example, my favourite sort of prayer—"So long as space remains, so long as sentient beings" suffering remains, I will remain in order to serve them." In order to develop such courageous determination you need a sense of strong self; in order to combat a self-centered negative attitude you need confidence and for that, sense of strong self is necessary. I think sense of strong self combined with ignorance or shortsightedness can become wrong. Okay?

QUESTION: *I am a neuroscientist from London and I have done research on the effect of meditation on the brain. One of my favorite photographs is a picture of you taking a photograph of someone going into a brain scanner. I use it to show that you are actually very happy to talk to neuroscientists about the impact of meditation and spirituality on the brain. But that photograph is quite a few years old. What are your thoughts at the moment on what neuroscientists can do to help us understand happiness?*

HIS HOLINESS: As I mentioned earlier, usually I am making an effort to promote awareness in these things in order to create individual happy persons, happy families, happy communities. If I use a reason based on quoting other people, it may not be universally acceptable. So I use a common experience, common sense, like scientific findings. Certain concepts of finding, through scientific research, are very much based on a valid sort of reasoning, because they prove it by experiment. Buddha had stated, "None of my followers—bhikshus or scholars or learned—should accept my teaching out of faith, out of devotion, but should rather investigate and experiment."

He said that; so we as Buddhists, particularly the followers of the Nalanda tradition, should really investigate even the Buddha's own word. Some words of the Buddha's go against the findings from investigation; they took the liberty to reject what the Buddha said. If we rely on a religious sort of belief, even if one religion is very popular, very important, it can never become universal. But scientific research and findings can be universal. So I feel, so far—I think in the last ten years—those scientists who really carry out experiments have been really very useful. My attempt at the promotion of inner value mainly uses common experience, common value and then scientific experiments.

So you are from that field—very good. Carry on more research and . . . I think you are of the Indian community? I think ancient Indian thought is very open, so a scientist from that background may become more successful. Your mind is not fixed and still open.

QUESTION: *Your Holiness, thank you very much for the inspiring talk. You talked a lot about compassion and happiness. I have a conflict in my mind—if I have compassion and if someone I love dearly is in pain, how can I keep myself happy?*

HIS HOLINESS: Shantideva, a great scholar from the eighth century and an Indian Buddhist master, had raised this question. Nobody wants anxiety or painful experiences or disturbances. But if you practice compassion very forcefully, very effectively, you may get some kind of disturbance. When you see someone passing through a painful experience, you also seem get some kind of disturbance and mental pain—so you have to make a distinction between yourself and him. Your own pain overwhelms you; it is a mental sort of pain, or even a physical pain or some kind of helplessness which has not occurred to you voluntarily.

But the discomfort you feel as a result of too much concern about others' well-being—that is voluntary. You trained yourself to develop that kind of responsibility; you gave yourself the courage to take care of others' well-being. If you are weak, it is impossible to take care of others' well-being. Too much thinking about others' well-being causes vast problems, because there is almost limitless suffering on this planet—within humanity or among other animals.

I think in India, traditionally, there has been a very good sort of culture of vegetarianism. I think that is really wonderful. In the early 1960s, when I was passing through from Dharamshala to Jammu Airport, there was almost no chicken selling. Nowadays, every sort of small restaurant sells chicken in the name of progress. In Bangalore, also, I noticed with vegetables there was some chicken. People treat chicken like vegetables. No feeling for their pain. During summer and winter, there are small chickens huddled in the cages—very sad.

I, myself, am non-vegetarian now, but I have some reasons. In 1965 or 1966, I gave up non-vegetarian food, including eggs. The next about—I think—twenty months, I remained very strictly vegetarian. During that period, according to advice from an Indian friend, I took a lot of cream and a lot of nuts; as a result, I got my gallbladder problem. Then, I think, for at least three to four weeks, I had really serious illness. My whole body—eyes and nails also—all became yellow. Later I expressed to some of my friends that, at that time, I truly became the living Buddha, completely yellow—not through spiritual practice but through illness.

So both the Tibetan physician and the allopathic physician advised me better to follow my original diet. So that is the struggle. That's my excuse. Actually, we are trying to promote vegetarianism, so I think we need a worldwide sort of movement. On some occasions, in Japan, I tease the Japanese for too much fishing. The worse thing is that some play with fish—they hook them and make them struggle, then release all fishes, injured in their mouth like that.

QUESTION: *Your Holiness, thank you for being with us; we are so obliged. I had a question—in our pursuit of happiness, we have all seen or heard of bad things. You know, like cruelty to animals—we read about it accidently in a book, or see it and in those moments, when these come to haunt us, we don't want to think about torture or pain to living creatures. How do we put an end to those thoughts? I mean, can we delete them, can we put an end to them, because those are negative thoughts?*

HIS HOLINESS: Two ways—think more on what really helps or benefits out of anger, hatred, or the desire to harm the other. Just the desire to harm the other may not actually harm them; only through action, you can harm. So if you really want to harm the other, without anger, and with a calm mind, analyze and find out about the other's weak spot and then hit. If you yourself are angry, you become a little bit mad. You cannot find the weak spot then, if you just hit. Then, sometimes, you give your own hand more pain.

So, for example, if we Tibetans here keep anger toward our troublemakers there, of course *they* would consider us to be the troublemakers. So we consider them the troublemakers. Anyway, you see that only the negative feeling won't harm them; instead, keep patience, keep compassion. In 2008, after the crisis of March 10, I had more or less the same experience that I had developed in 1959—helplessness, too much sort of anxiety, fear. But during the 2008 crisis, I deliberately kept on the practice of give and take. Visualize some of those hardliner Chinese officials, take their anger, their fear, and give them my sort of spirit of forgiveness and compassion. Immense help—not in solving the problem but in keeping my mind calm and compassionate.

So, like that, if you let anger destroy your peace of mind, it will eventually ruin your own health. So keep compassion—your mind will remain clear. If you develop full compassion, not let anger or hatred in, then after constant effort for days and months and years, decades, your mental state can change, that much I can tell you through my own little experience.

QUESTION: *I am a medical doctor. Twenty years ago, I asked you what we should do as doctors but now my question is: How can we help the patient keep his happiness when he is ill? What is the attitude of the patient toward life when he is ill?*

HIS HOLINESS: Depends on their mental attitude. If anyone believes in God, that we are creatures of God, and that God means infinite love, they see that in their illness there is some meaning. Then, those people who believe in law of causality will believe that today's unfortunate things—including illness—are due to your own past negative karma. However, every experience is due to previous karma; even serious illness is due to some serious negative karma. Still that karma is your own creation; therefore, if you create another, stronger positive karma, then the effect of that negative karma will reduce. So, ultimately, you have some control.

Then, perhaps, a nonbeliever, when faced with some problem or painful experience, will analyze the situation. If the situation is such that you can overcome, then, no need to worry or make effort. If the situation is such that it cannot be overcome, then no need for too much worry also. Too much worry is self-torture; it is better to forget. Not easy, but that is, I think, a very realistic approach when we face some problem.

Here is my own little experience. I think more than ten years ago, I developed some sort of pain in my intestines. That day I was in Bihar, passing through a village; I saw a lot of poor people, poor children without shoes or any opportunity for education. Very sad. Then, I saw worse things in Patna. Then when I reached my own hotel, the pain developed, and almost the whole night I experienced pain. But I constantly thought of these helpless children. When my mind was diverted out of sense of karuna—of compassion—my own physical pain reduced. So think more about others' well-being than your own problems, including your own sickness. Otherwise, I don't know, I think you have to consult with some kind of western psychologist or psychiatrist or so on. Or maybe the best thing is alcohol? Or, just lie down.

QUESTION: *I was wondering whether the request for not raising any political questions comes from His Holiness or from the organizers*

25

of this wonderful lecture—in the sense that doesn't politics have an impact on happiness in our times as in other times? That aside, is justice a constituent of the compassion that you talk about? Could you elaborate on it a bit?

HIS HOLINESS: I think justice is on the level of action, and compassion is a motivation. Motivation, such as compassion, is really about taking care of others' well-being. With that kind of mental attitude there will be no place to lie, to exploit or harm, because you are very much taking care about their well-being.

For example, Buddhist monastic practice mentions, when a monk witnessed a hunter approach an animal, it disappears into the forest; the monk noticed in which direction. When the hunter comes and asks the monk where that animal had gone, if the monk tells truth, the hunter will catch the animal. In such circumstances, it is better to tell a lie, because the motivation is sincere. So it is permitted. So lying is at the action level—physical action, mental action, whether positive or negative.

The other day, one Vietnamese group asked me about corruption in order to get good jobs for the community or for a bigger number of workers. I told them that such a purpose, with sincere, compassionate motivation, stems from the concern of larger group of people. If it involves some little bit of corruption, then it is positive corruption. So these things depend on purpose and motivation like that.

Politics, actually, you see, I am now already retired from political responsibility as far as the Tibet struggle is concerned. I voluntarily, happily, proudly handed over to our elected political leadership. So these days, if someone asks me some sort of complicated political question regarding the Chinese, then I usually say I am now retired. So I have more freedom—if I want to answer, I answer, and if I do not want, I say I am retired.

QUESTION: *With all gratitude and humility, I want to know what your definition is of God and how does one experience God?*

HIS HOLINESS: One time, I think in the West, some reporter asked me, "If you had the opportunity to see Jesus Christ, what would your question be?" I answered, "What is God?" (*Laughs*) So it is mystery. Of course, I think every religion has one sort of terminology, but certain things are beyond our thought, beyond our words, inconceivable. Buddha was an enlightened human being.

But then, the very detailed sort of enlightenment, the highest sort of mental quality is beyond our thought. It is difficult. I think that modern science has neither proof nor disproof regarding God. It is a mystery.

2

DIFFERENT LEVELS OF HAPPINESS

New Delhi, 2011

B rothers and sisters, I'm extremely happy to be once more in this hall. On the previous occasion there were some pigeons flying here and there, but today it seems there are no longer any pigeons . . .

Firstly, since this is the thirtieth anniversary of Tushita, I must say to Zopa Rinpoche and his organization that during the last thirty years you have really offered a lot of service to the Buddhadharma, and through that I think a certain number of people have got some more inner peace. So, I appreciate that.

Now, some years have passed since my last talk in this hall. Time never stands still; it is always moving, and no force can stop that. But what we can do is use time properly. In what sense do I mean "properly"? I think that even these flowers have a certain right to grow, to blossom, and also eventually to produce a seed, ensuring another generation. On top of this physical element, we, as living beings, as sentient beings, have this mysterious thing that we call the "mind" or "consciousness," as well as emotions. Although the grosser levels of consciousness and emotions are very much based on brain cells, the ultimate nature of consciousness is still something mysterious for ordinary people.

Obviously, everybody has a feeling of self—of "I." For the last three thousand years or so, human beings have been trying to identify what the self is, so there are different views of the self. Also, everybody has the experience of pleasure and pain, and every animal also has a similar sort of experience. So, with freedom of the self and experiences of pleasure and pain, it is natural for one to desire to get more pleasure, more happiness, and to not want suffering. That feeling is common to all sentient beings, despite different physical characteristics. It is obvious that cats, dogs, and other animals, including even small insects, all have a feeling of I, of self, and with that a desire to have less suffering.

Now, here, when I use the word "happiness," I'm talking about happiness in the sense of genuine, deep satisfaction. It can also happen that physical hardships or difficulties can bring more satisfaction. I think that, to some extent, animals can also experience that kind of satisfaction. The difference between us human beings and other animals is our unique human intelligence, and it is because of that that we have different levels of satisfaction. For animals, I think, satisfaction comes mainly from physical or sensory experiences. We human beings share that same level of satisfaction with other animals, but because of our unique intelligence, because the human mind is much more sophisticated, we have greater satisfaction on the mental level. Although animals do, to some extent, experience both sensory and mental levels of satisfaction, we human beings clearly experience greater satisfaction on the mental level.

Now, people such as athletes sometimes really experience much hardship on the physical level. But they have a certain goal and when they achieve that goal they have tremendous satisfaction on the mental level. So, all the hardship on the physical level brings then more satisfaction. I think we even have our own experiences of this. For example, there can be two patients with the same sort of physical illness in the same sort of room in the same hospital. One has mentally more ability to think certain different things; the other has less of that mental ability and is only concerned about their physical experiences. The patient with less mental ability to think about things will have more pain and more frustration. Although the level of physical pain is similar, the mental level, their different attitudes to their illness and to pain, makes a difference.

Of course, sometimes we say, "Today my body is a little uncomfortable, a little painful, but my mind is very happy." And there can be the opposite case, with no problem physically but mentally being unhappy. Obviously, there are two levels. Now, between these two, which is more serious? It's the mental level. Physical illness or discomfort can be subdued by mental happiness. Mental satisfaction can subdue physical pain. On the other hand, if a person is mentally unhappy, with too much worry, too much stress, physical comfort cannot subdue that mental anxiety. The mental level is more important.

Now, as to the different levels of happiness or satisfaction, at a very basic level, I can say that I am happy. Since I had a very good sleep last night followed by a good breakfast and a good lunch, I'm very happy, very satisfied. That kind of happiness, or satisfaction, is common with other animals. When animals are well fed and in no immediate danger, they just remain very peaceful. I think they can also meditate in that way. When a rabbit sits without moving, I think it's meditating. And it's the same with a pigeon, when it's well fed and in no immediate danger. Actually, of course, meditation is much more sophisticated than that. Just closing your eyes and not moving is not meditation.

There is another level of happiness that is not related to the physical level. For example, in my own case, I feel happy if, during the last month or last year, I did some useful sort of work, such as taking part in meetings or doing my own study or practice, which gives me some kind of satisfaction, or if I fulfilled the real meaning of life by offering a little service to others. If I'm able to bring some temporary happiness or satisfaction to others, including animals, I feel happy.

Just two days ago, when I was coming from the airport to my hotel and had to stop at a red light, I noticed one small, very poor girl on the street. That girl was begging, with one glass, from the people driving cars. Fortunately, my car stopped at that place. Because of my previous experience of such incidents, I usually keep some money in my bag, but the other day I had nothing in it except a few sweets. I then borrowed some money from one of the officials in my car and gave it to that young girl. An hour before, I had received a milk chocolate from a friend, so I also gave her that. At that moment I just felt happy. Her mother then came along carrying another smaller child and that young girl gave her mother a big smile. At that moment, as soon as I saw the young girl's joyful attitude toward her mother, I really felt a deep satisfaction. So, small things can bring some kind of joyfulness, at least for a short period of time.

When I reflect on these things, I see that there is another level of happiness or satisfaction that has nothing to do with the physical. Of course, my spiritual experience is very, very limited— maybe a little above zero. When I reflect on these things, I see that there can be deep satisfaction on a purely mental level without needing to rely on the senses—on seeing, hearing, tasting or touching something. That satisfaction gives me more enthusiasm to carry these kinds of practices further and also a desire to share them with other people who are mentally confused.

We have daily experiences of different levels of happiness. I think that nonbelievers also have the same kinds of experiences from helping or serving others, or from at least not harming them. Helping others gives you a happy feeling and through such attitudes you get more friends. Wherever you go, you see more smiles, more friendliness. If you yourself are extremely self-centered and narrow-minded, you are suspicious of others, and because of your self-centeredness, you remain distant from others. With such feelings, it's impossible for you to feel happy when you see more people; you feel uncomfortable. So that's actually against basic human nature. We are social animals.

Throughout an individual's life, having a happy life depends on others; it's the very basis of a happy, successful life. If you are suspicious and remain at a distance from others, you become mentally isolated; then you feel loneliness, fear, and a sense of insecurity. So, no matter whether you are a believer or a nonbeliever, be an honest, warm-hearted person; you will then be a much happier person. That's very important. We are not talking here about the next life or God or Buddha. We are simply investigating the best way to achieve a happy life, and these inner attitudes, these inner qualities, are the key factors to being a happy person.

Since we are social animals, we are part of a society, and in order to live happily in that society, it is essential that we have community spirit, that we share problems and other things, and fully cooperate with each other. The community will then be much happier. In order to achieve genuine cooperation, friendship is the key factor, and trust is the basis of friendship, not money, power, education, or intelligence. If there is real trust, friendship comes then. If you have trust, warm-heartedness and a genuine concern for the well-being of others, taking as much care of others as you do of yourself, there is then no room for cheating others, for anger or jealousy.

If someone is successful, you should feel happy rather than concerned that they are becoming more successful than you. There should be no room for jealousy or for negative competitive feelings. Positive competitive feelings are good, but negative ones are not. As long as you respect others' rights, as long as you have genuine concern for others' well-being, there is no room for killing, stealing, lying, rape, or bullying. All your conduct, all your physical, verbal, and mental actions can be transparent.

Genuine openness and warm-heartedness are the basis of self-confidence, of inner strength. With them, you can deal with other people transparently, as you have nothing to hide. That's the basis of developing trust. Trust brings friendship, and friendship brings a happy community, or even a happy family. Whether you accept religious faith or not is up to the individual; it's the individual's business. But what I call "secular ethics" is necessary because we want a happy life. We are not talking about the next life or other things. Simply, we want a happy life.

On the other level, there are believers. I feel these are two aspects to all the major religious traditions—one aspect is practice and the other is philosophy or theory. As far as the aspect of practice is concerned, all major religious traditions are the same. All the traditions teach us the practices of love and compassion, and with that, the spirit of forgiveness and tolerance, as well as self-discipline.

Now, in order to boost these practices, different philosophies and different views happened. There are two religious groups—theistic and non-theistic. The theistic religious group believes in a powerful creator, whether God or Allah or Brahma, and ultimately, everything depends on this creator. All of existence and particularly human beings were created by the same God.

On one occasion in Jerusalem, I met and had a discussion with some Jews and some Palestinian Muslims. One Jewish schoolteacher told our gathering something he taught the Palestinian students in his class. When the Palestinian students see Israeli soldiers or police at checkpoints, they usually feel unhappy. So he suggested that when they faced someone who irritated them, they should remember that person is in the image of God. This is what he taught them, and later some of the Palestinian students reported that they found immense benefit in following his advice. On the mental level, their feelings of discomfort were immediately reduced. In that way, if you have tremendous faith in God, when you face people who usually cause you uncomfortable irritation, you can think, "This person is in the image of God. He is also created by God." That's a very powerful method.

On one occasion in America or in Canada, I sat together with a Christian and after we had discussed and exchanged some spiritual values, he played a guitar and sang some kind of praise to God. Meanwhile, tears came from his eyes because of his tremendous faith in God. Actually, that total submission to God also acts to reduce self-centered ego. In the Buddhist approach, there are two types of selflessness—one, the selflessness of conventional life and the other, the ultimate level of selflessness; the aim is to reduce extreme self-centered ego. So, tremendous faith in God and submission to God act in more or less the same way. Also, God is infinite love, so believers themselves then have to follow that example. So that is very good. These practices are on the mental, not the sensory level.

I think you can utilize the sensory level to complement the mental level—by listening to religious music or seeing a religious picture, for example. For me, I see statues or pictures of Mary carrying Jesus Christ as a young baby as a very significant symbol of love or compassion. It is very beautiful. But Jesus Christ on the cross sometimes makes me feel sad. Mary carrying the young baby Jesus is related to compassion, love, kindness. One time I went on a pilgrimage to a Christian holy place, Fatima, in Portugal, where there is a small statue of Mary. A few of us were there, along with, of course, local Christian brothers and sisters. We sat together for a few moments of silent meditation. After we stood up and were about to leave, I turned back to look at the statue. That small statue of Mary was actually smiling at me. I thought that there was something wrong with my mind, but when I later reflected on the incident, I decided that it was real.

I had had a similar kind of experience one time in a Tibetan monastery in south India. I really have much admiration for Mary, so I think Mary appreciated that, or gave me some kind of special blessing. Or sometimes I jokingly say that Mary didn't make a distinction between Buddhists and non-Buddhists. Actually, Buddhism has no concept of a creator. Strictly speaking, from the theistic religious viewpoint, Buddhists are nonbelievers.

Anyway, if there is faith, certain theories held by all the different major traditions are very good because they provide inner peace, peace on the mental level. With regard to non-theistic religious traditions, there are Buddhism, Jainism, and Sankhya, another ancient Indian non-Buddhist school of thought which is very sophisticated and a most effective opponent in the philosophical field to Buddhism. It is a very rich, very sophisticated philosophy. In the Sankhya tradition, there are two groups: one group accepts a creator and the other does not.

The non-theistic traditions do not believe in a creator but believe in the law of causality—that things come into being as the continuation of previous causes and conditions. It is not that everything suddenly happens with no cause. There is no creator; everything happens due to its own causes and conditions, so we call that the law of causality. According to that, as I mentioned before, with regard to any positive action, "positive" means not only bringing some temporary satisfaction to yourself but long-term satisfaction or benefit, which comes through serving others. Bringing some benefit to others is the best way to gain long-term satisfaction for yourself, because that's positive action—positive karma. Positive karma brings a positive result.

Examples of negative karma are such things as killing, stealing, sexual misconduct (mainly rape), telling lies, harming others' bodies and material possessions, divisive talk which involves words that divide friends or people who are about to come together. We usually say that there are ten negative karmas, and opposite to them are the positive karmas, such as refraining from harming others, refraining from killing, refraining from stealing, and so on. Karma means action. Practitioners who believe in the theory of karma sometimes easily blame: "Oh, this is due to karma! Nothing can be done!" I think that is a mistake. Karma is created by us, so in case we are about to experience the result of some negative karma—if we make the effort—through our effort we can create stronger positive karma that can neutralize the previous negative karma. Through the sheer force of the positive karma, the potential of the negative karma to produce negative consequences can be eliminated.

When you reflect on your right actions—the actions that bring at least some happiness, some satisfaction, some comfort to others, including animals—you get tremendous satisfaction. This happens at the mental level, and it happens according to the law of karma. So, karma can change, because it is your own creation. Everything depends on your own willpower—"I must do this, no matter how many obstacles there are." Even though a few years ago you felt it was impossible that you could practice certain things, as time passes and you familiarize yourself with those things, your mind gradually comes closer and closer and closer. After a few decades, you actually experience those things.

In my own case, a few decades ago, there were certain things that I felt were difficult to actually practice, but now, after thirty or forty years, such things have become much, much easier. It's the same subject, the same person, the same mind, but because of getting used to the practice, it gets closer and closer. It is like with astronauts. They cannot manage everything at once, but through training and becoming familiar with what they have to do, they eventually can do it without much thinking. Turning on the first switch, the second switch, the third switch, comes automatically.

Buddhist literature mentions that there is a limitation to any physical training. Because the physical level is grosser, there is limitation. Through training you can jump some remarkable distance or height, but there's still limitation. But since the mind is formless, if you make it familiar with certain things, there's no limitation. It can be increased, because the basis is not solid. With physical training, because the basis is solid, there's limitation. But for a mental quality, once you develop it to a certain level, as long as you remember the development, that feeling automatically comes. There's no need to put in effort in each case. But with physical training, as for example with athletes, you need to train continuously. If you don't exercise for a few months, you need to train again to reach that same level. The mental quality is not like that. Through our own experiences, if we pay attention, we will notice there are differences between the qualities of the physical and mental levels.

Our mind is formless, shapeless, and while in one way it is very difficult to control, in another way it is very easy to control, to transform. Control or transformation at the mental level comes about entirely through voluntary willingness, through enthusiasm. No external force can change our minds; it can only be changed voluntarily. So in order to develop that kind of voluntary enthusiasm, you must see the benefit of certain positive ways of thinking, such as loving, kindness, respect for others and rejoicing in others' good activities, and the harmfulness of anger, jealousy, and other negative minds. That is what brings the conviction: "I want to reduce these negative emotions and increase the positive ones." You then voluntarily make effort in that.

Once you see the necessity of that kind of transformation, you then develop the willpower to carry out the effort day and night, including in your dreams. This formless, shapeless mind will then gradually change. The sources of your anxiety and mental troubles will ultimately be reduced, and your peace of mind will increase no matter what is happening around you. No external force can ever destroy our inner peace. Our inner peace is immediately destroyed by our own inner enemies—anger, hatred, jealousy. These are the real enemy. An external enemy, no matter how powerful, can only destroy your physical body, not your peace of mind. It is the internal enemy that destroys our inner peace. Once anger, hatred, or jealousy develops, it immediately destroys our inner peace. So, the enemy is not outside; the enemy is here inside.

One of my Muslim friends said that "jihad" actually means to struggle with destructive emotions—what Buddhists call the inner enemy. That's one meaning of jihad. So all these practices actually entail the concept of jihad. But some people have a different impression of its meaning.

From the viewpoint of a Buddhist practitioner, the more you gain of inner experience, the more stable your mind becomes. Of course, as I mentioned earlier, I myself am a very poor practitioner, but even from my small experience I can assure you that through training the mind, your mind becomes more stable and experiences less stress and less fear, which brings more self-confidence. Also, with a calm mind we can see reality more clearly. When our mind is dominated by fear, anxiety, or anger, we cannot see reality properly. The very thing that tries to look at reality somehow distorts it so that you cannot see it. When our mind is very disturbed, we cannot utilize our human intelligence properly. I think that warm-heartedness immediately brings inner strength and also enables our mind to function more normally, more objectively. In that way you gain another level of peace of mind, another level of happiness or satisfaction.

If you train in that way, even when you have been born as a very ordinary person, there's a possibility that at the time of death, your mental state will be more advanced. There is then a one hundred percent guarantee that your next life will be a very positive one. Life after life will be that way. Buddhists believe that for limitless aeons life can be better, better, better, better, until the final destination of Buddhahood is reached. The maximum happiness is that at Buddhahood.

In the Heart Sutra is the Sanskrit mantra: *Tadyatha gate gate paragate parasamgate bodhi svaha*. Of course, I cannot pronounce it properly. When real scholars of Sanskrit chant in Sanskrit, it is remarkable. With the Tibetan tongue, I don't know. Anyway, the meaning of *tadyatha* is "it is thus"; *gate gate* means "go, go"; *paragate* means "go beyond"; *parasamgate* means "go perfectly beyond"; and *bodhi svaha* means "may the seed of Bodhi, or enlightenment, be planted."

Usually, I jokingly tell people that *gate gate paragate parasamgate bodhi svaha* has two levels—one physical and the other mental. On the physical level, without our effort, we go, go, go beyond, which means we go from being a child to being a youth and then to middle age and to being old. Then with *bodhi svaha*, we are finally in the cemetery. On one occasion, in either Europe or America, we had to pass through a nearby cemetery. Afterward, in my talk, I mentioned that experience of passing through the cemetery, and that it's our final destination. On the physical level, there's no need of effort; it happens automatically.

My stage is now *parasamgate*. Since I'm now seventy-six, *gate gate* and *paragate* have already gone, and now it's *parasamgate*, with the cemetery as the only final destination. Or perhaps my body will be put in a chorten, or stupa, I don't know. But anyway, that's the final destination on the physical level. So, effortlessly it goes that way.

Now, where we need to apply effort is at the mental level of *gate gate paragate parasamgate bodhi svaha*. The first two, *gate gate*, refer to the paths of accumulation and preparation. *Paragate* means having reached the third level, the path of seeing. And according to the Bodhisattvayana stages, the first bhumi is then reached, followed by the rest of the ten bhumis. After that comes *bodhi svaha*—Buddhahood. As I mentioned earlier, I'm a small Buddhist practitioner, and I'm really making the effort of going the way of *gate gate*. Sometimes I feel some signs of the first *gate*; although I haven't reached there, I already have some signs of it. So, if I have more time to make an effort, I'm quite sure that I will reach that first level of *gate*.

Basically we are all the same, the same human beings. Mentally, emotionally, and physically we are same. Then, from the Buddhist viewpoint, everybody has Buddha-nature, or *Tathagatagarbha*. The Buddha-nature, or Buddha-seed, is there. As long as the clear light is there, the Buddha-seed is there. Clear light is the ultimate source, the ultimate cause of consciousness. So as long as consciousness is there, the ultimate source of consciousness must be there. That, roughly speaking, is Buddha-nature. That is the potential to become all-knowing. From that, enlightenment comes. Stones, which are mindless, have no Buddha-nature, so they don't have that potential. Sentient beings, even animals, have consciousness. Even though an animal's consciousness is very limited, the consciousness is still there. Therefore, since from the Buddhist viewpoint, all sentient beings have Buddha-nature, there is always the possibility for them to achieve Buddhahood.

So, with regard to the different levels of happiness, nonbelievers achieve it on a secular basis. That is one thing. Secondly, for believers, there are theistic religious beliefs and non-theistic religious beliefs. Buddhism comes within non-theistic religious beliefs, and within Buddhism there are also the Pali and the Sanskrit traditions.

So, as I usually do, I want to take some questions. But I want to make it clear that they should be meaningful questions, not silly ones. Silly questions are a waste of time. And if there are too many silly questions I may get irritated, and then you will get some scolding. That will also be a good demonstration of the Dalai Lama's anger.

Questions

QUESTION: *How does a child find happiness when seeing a parent suffering a terminal illness?*

HIS HOLINESS: I fully share your concern. It makes me think of when my own mother passed away, and particularly of when my Senior Tutor passed away. When my Senior Tutor, who gave me full ordination as a monk, passed away, I really felt I'd lost a solid rock on which I leaned. At the time of his passing, I no longer had that solid rock. But then I remembered that my late tutor often used to recite Shantideva's verse of advice—when we're passing through some difficulties, we have to think about the reality of those difficulties. If there's the possibility of overcoming them, then there's no need to worry; and if there's no way to overcome that sort of tragedy, then there's no use in worrying. It's a very realistic approach.

So, when you are facing a situation where your parent has a terminal illness—a very serious or painful disease—please make every effort to overcome that, to have it cured. If it's impossible to cure it, then take care of yourself more. And even if the worst outcome happens, you should lead your life in a more meaningful way so that your late parent would feel happy. If you worry too much, and in the worst case have a nervous breakdown due to too much anxiety, I think your friends would feel very sad, as would your late parent. After the death of my tutor, I said to myself, "Now I *must* take full responsibility to fulfill my late tutor's wishes." So that tragedy translated into gaining more strength, more enthusiasm.

If you are a nonbeliever, think about doing things in this life. If you are a believer who believes in future lives, you can do the recitation of certain mantras and dedicate that to your parent. And if you're a believer in a theistic religion, remember God and remember that there must be some meaning in your parent's sad situation. Only God knows that meaning; you don't. If you believe in the law of karma, think about your parent's own karma and about how this particular result has flourished out of their previous karma.

QUESTION: *How can we love those people who don't love us?*

HIS HOLINESS: Our love is usually a biased love. That love is actually attachment, and that is not healthy. Attachment goes very much along with hatred and jealousy. What we need is unbiased love and compassion, unconditional love and compassion. If the reason you love someone is that he or she loves you or is good to you, that's biased love. Irrespective of whether or not someone is positive toward you, that person deserves your compassion, your concern. This includes your enemy. As far as their attitude is concerned, someone might be negative toward you, but you don't think about that; you think that your enemy is also a sentient being and also wants happiness and has every right to overcome suffering. In this way, you develop a genuine sense of concern for their well-being. That is unbiased compassion, real compassion. In order to develop that, we must practice on a basis of detachment, then equalize ourselves with every other sentient being, both friends and enemies. From seeing that everyone has the same right to overcome suffering, we then develop a sense of concern. That's unbiased love; that's real love.

If you can practice that, then practice it; if not, then make some preparation for revenge—I'm joking! Revenge brings more irritation, more disturbance. If you fail and respond forcefully, you will have even more worry, limitless worry. Right from the beginning, open yourself, thinking, "It doesn't matter what they do." Of course, if they try to harm you physically, be careful. You must be careful, otherwise you will think or say something negative. Just think, "It doesn't matter, it doesn't matter."

For example, when some Chinese officials describe me as a demon, it makes me laugh. I sometimes jokingly tell some of my Chinese friends that the more they repeat that accusation, the longer and longer my demon horns grow. It's just silly, isn't it? So, think in that way, take it easy and there will be no problem.

QUESTION: *What is the role of karma and emotions in the pursuit of happiness?*

HIS HOLINESS: I think strong desire might also be a kind of emotion in that sense, but there is an important role played by strong positive emotions, such as tremendous compassion, a feeling of concern for others' suffering. When you think of others' sufferings, tears come out because there is so much feeling, but that emotion is very positive emotion, bringing more enthusiasm to serve others, to do something for others. That kind of emotion brings determination, as expressed in my favorite prayer—"As long as space remains, as long as sentient beings' suffering remains,

I will remain in order to serve them." That kind of powerful determination is brought about by such emotions.

So, emotion is not necessarily negative. I think there are two kinds of emotion. One type of emotion comes spontaneously and is generally destructive. Another type of emotion comes through training, through reasoning and familiarization, and is usually positive.

QUESTION: *How can parents help their children to be happy?*

HIS HOLINESS: I think it depends on the children's age. In my own experience, when I was very young, I remember that whenever a new person came to British India's consulate in Lhasa, he would always bring a toy for me. When I received the information that a new person had come and wanted an official meeting, I was always excited about what kind of toy he would give me. So, at a very young age, that is what is important. When children have grown up a little, I think they need meaningful guidance or examples. At all ages, it is your maximum affection, maximum love for your children that's very important. I think the strongest instrument in changing another's mind is love, not money.

Genuine affection and a genuine sense of concern really affect the minds and emotions of children.

QUESTION: *Your Holiness said that one should be fearless, but if your parents put fear in your mind, you can't oppose them.*

HIS HOLINESS: That depends on the motivation, and also on the goal. If your children are a little lazy, if you have a good purpose and sincere concern for their future well-being, you can sometimes use a little pressure or threat. Such things are positive. It's not good to look down on your children and tease them or be sarcastic. You must respect your children and provide them with maximum affection.

Here I'll tell you a story about me. When I was seven or eight, I had already started learning by heart some of the root texts. Because my mind was quite sharp, I could easily learn by heart, but because of that, I was also very lazy. At that time my elder brother and I were studying together, so my tutor kept two whips, one yellow one and one ordinary one. The ordinary whip was for my elder brother; and the yellow whip was supposed to be the holy whip for the holy student—the Dalai Lama. So I know that the holy whip doesn't produce holy pain, just ordinary pain. Out of my fear, I put a little more effort into learning. But later, of course, my tutor was very kind. Some of my effort was out of fear; but my effort out of deep appreciation for their sense of concern for me and their love was much, much stronger.

As I mentioned earlier, when my tutor passed away, I really felt a tremendous loss, so that was for that very person who kept a whip. So, that's the example. You must provide maximum affection and occasionally, if it's necessary, you can use methods or words that are a little harsh, but you do so out of a genuine sense of concern and for a good purpose. You must act according to the circumstances.

QUESTION: *Can happiness reduce corruption in society and a nation?*

HIS HOLINESS: Yes, genuine happiness on the basis of honesty and truth. The people who feel that you get satisfaction with the more money you make through actions not based on moral ethics are wrong. That's very, very superficial thinking; they're actually foolish and short-sighted. Corrupt people—whether religious leaders, businessmen, politicians, or from any other profession—are actually weak deep inside, and their lives are full of illusion. Such people cannot act transparently because they have something to hide; because of that very fact, an uncomfortable feeling is always there deep inside. How can they be transparent? They cannot. As I mentioned earlier, they cannot build real trust, and they eventually become lowly. Corrupt people are very foolish, very short-sighted.

QUESTION: *What is the role of music in bringing peace in the world?*

HIS HOLINESS: I must say that it is very limited. Of course, as I mentioned earlier, a certain satisfaction comes at the sensory level. Things like music and beautiful scenery can bring some peace of mind, but that kind of peace of mind is entirely dependent on external factors; and when those factors are not there, you find it difficult to pass the time. I sometimes feel a little pity for some groups of tourists. Some old people have a lot of money, but since they are retired and have no particular job, they lack some kind of thinking power. To experience some satisfaction they're entirely dependent on the sensory level. Unless they have some occupation at the external sensory level, they can't pass the time; they're bored. If you have some experience of peace of mind and satisfaction at the mental level, you don't need to depend on the sense faculties. You don't need to go here and there. You can just stay in solitude and think; you get maximum peace of mind.

On one occasion I visited a big monastery in Barcelona, in Spain. One Spanish Catholic monk came to see me and the organizer told me that the monk had spent five years in solitude on the mountain behind that monastery. He remained there for such a long period, five years with almost no hot meals. When we met, I said to him, "I was told you spent five years in the mountains as a hermit. What kind of practice did you do on the mountain?" He told me, "I meditated on love." When he mentioned that, in his eyes there was a certain reflection of his warm-heartedness. I developed a deep respect and admiration for him.

Another thing was that his English was even worse than mine. I was fond of speaking in my broken English to him because my English was a little better than his. We had a very meaningful conversation. That was a wonderful monk.

Some Buddhist practitioners, including some Tibetans, also prefer to remain in very lonely, isolated places because it gives them the opportunity to utilize their human abilities at the mental level, bringing them tremendous inner peace and inner strength. Such people never rely on music or other external things. Of course, hearing music can supplement other spiritual practice. Sometimes we can just think about the meaning of a certain prayer, and at other times hearing that same prayer with a certain tune can affect us more. All religious traditions combine certain prayers with music. I think the main thing is practice at the mental level, but you can see things, hear songs, and also sometimes have a blessed pill put in your mouth. So all these three senses can work together as a supplement for mental practice.

QUESTION: *Who has got more power to love and be affectionate—a man or a woman?*

HIS HOLINESS: I think, generally, due to biological factors, the female has more capacity with regard to a sense of concern for others' well-being. In one discussion I had with scientists, they stated that when two people—one male and one female—look at someone who is experiencing pain, the female's response is stronger than the male's. Also, biologically, with the male, once he's enjoyed himself it's finished; but the female has to carry the child for many months, and then after birth she has to make tremendous effort to take care of the child.

I often tell the story of something I noticed on a long night flight I once took from Japan to America. Among the passengers I noticed one young couple with two children. One child was very small and the other could walk. At the beginning, the older child was running here and there, creating a little disturbance, but it didn't matter. At the beginning, both parents were looking after the two children. Then, about midnight, the father just went to sleep. The mother was still caring for those two kids. She took care of them, particularly the younger one, the whole night. By the time we had almost reached San Francisco or Los Angeles, the mother's eyes had become very red. That's one clear indication. Both parents really loved their children, but there was some limitation to the father's taking care of them, whereas the mother took care of them the whole night.

And look at birds and dogs. The mother continuously takes care of the youngsters until they become independent. With dogs, of course, the father just enjoys, then he's finished; he does nothing. But some birds stay together until their youngsters become independent, with both the father and mother feeding them. And then again, the mother has much stronger emotions toward the youngsters; that's a biological factor, because we need that. Our life starts and we survive with our mother's affection and our mother's milk. As I often tell people, there are a few hundred people in this hall, for example, and while we might be outwardly the same, I think those people who received maximum affection from their mothers when they were very young feel much safer, much calmer deep inside. Those individuals who lost their mothers, didn't receive affection from them or were even abused by them, though they are outwardly the same and might have a successful life, deep inside there is some pain, some trace of that experience.

Therefore, biologically, the female is more compassionate. When I give a public talk in America, Europe, or also in India, I usually mention that in the very early period, we human beings had no concept of leadership. Everybody was equal and worked together. Some Marxist philosophers say that that is the original Marxism—everybody was equal, working together and sharing whatever they got. Then eventually the concept of leadership came. At that time education played no role, so physical strength was the main factor in becoming the leader. So that was the beginning of male dominance. It is like this with other animals, like monkeys. Since the males are stronger, they became dominant.

Then eventually, education came to play a more important role in society, so that made for more equality. In recent years, recent centuries, there have been some very famous, effective female leaders. It also happened in this country; and Golda Meir in Israel was a very strong leader, wasn't she? That has brought a little more equality. Now the time has come when mere education is not sufficient. We need to put in special effort to promote and increase human compassion. Now, here, females should have a more active role. That's my general view. When it comes to the level of the individual family, I don't know. Sometimes, if the female has more ability, the father becomes like a slave. And sometimes, the mother becomes almost like a slave. It varies from case to case. But actually, as again I mentioned earlier, relationships should be based on genuine love, genuine compassion; they shouldn't be based on just physical attraction, but on deep respect for the other person. So, when you have genuine feelings of closeness and concern, on the basis of deep respect, the partners naturally become more equal. This always happens.

QUESTION: *When you see someone harming or destroying your environment, how do you reach out to them? How do you react to that situation?*

His Holiness: Does this refer to an individual family or to an organization? Nowadays some organizations, including governments, sometimes act according to their own plans. This applies particularly to countries like China, where there is no independent judiciary. But it can also apply to private businesses and to individual families.

If possible, it is sensible to talk to the person who has created that environmental problem. Taking care of the environment is in everybody's interest, and we can all also make small contributions to global ecology. For example, in my own case, I have never used the bathtub in a hotel during the past few decades; I only take a shower. I consider that one small contribution I have made to saving water. Of course, there's not much effect from just one person doing this. And whenever I leave a room, I always switch off all the lights. Those kinds of activities on the part of one individual don't have much significance, but at least mentally I have made some contribution. An individual family can take care of the environment by picking up rubbish. In small ways they can make a contribution, indirectly reducing global warming. So, educate your neighbor, and if that has no effect, get more people to jointly make some effort. If that fails, then I don't know—maybe fight!

QUESTION: *How can we really be happy in adverse or hostile circumstances?*

HIS HOLINESS: That entirely depends on your own inner strength. At the early stages this is difficult even for a practitioner, but we have to make the effort. Eventually you gain more inner strength, and it then becomes much easier to deal with such problems. Naturally, these practices are not easy. You need continuity of effort, with determination—"I *must* practice this. I *must* increase my compassion." Tolerance, or patience, will then automatically come. This is a realistic approach to patience and of immense help in bringing it. I think we usually neglect these basic elements of the mind and some destructive emotion becomes dominant.

Those people who believe in dharma or some other spiritual tradition, as I mentioned earlier—whether a theistic or a non-theistic religion—you should be sincere and serious about your own faith. That's important. Faith is not just lip service. Faith must become part of your daily life, then its real value comes. Those who don't have much belief in such traditions can simply think, "I want a happy life, and gaining a happy life depends on my inner strength, and that depends on my views, my attitudes."

So first, try to pay more attention to your inner values, besides just thinking about money, money, money, money. That is very superficial. Nowadays, when I listen to the BBC on the radio or watch television, they're always talking about dollar, dollar, economy, economy. I think that actually influences our minds to become more deluded. Out of the Egyptian, Chinese, and Indus Valley civilizations, I think the Indus Valley civilization developed much more sophisticated philosophical views. India has traditionally had a very strong, very rich inner science. Modern science is now paying more and more attention to and desiring to get more information about the mind and how to deal with emotions from India's traditional cultural heritage. It is very, very important to realize India's own ancient treasure and not neglect these inner values. Of course, it's very important to learn how to develop materially through modern science and technology, so education related to these things is also very, very important; but in the meantime, you must know traditional values. We Tibetans must also learn about modern education, but our own traditional values are still very much relevant. That is what I want to share with you. Thank you.

COMMENT: *Your Holiness, there's a message for you. I quote: "Your Holiness, I'm from Lhasa, and I think I can represent most Tibetan students. I want to say we love you, we respect you, we will follow you. You are the great master in our mind, in our heart."*

HIS HOLINESS: Thank you.

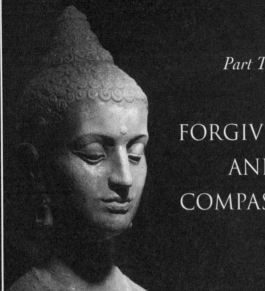

Part Two

FORGIVENESS
AND
COMPASSION

1

The Power of Forgiveness

Limerick, 2011

Thank you, thank you, thank you. I think, as a sign of respect, I will speak standing up. That way, I can also see more faces. I usually describe all of us as brothers and sisters. We are the same human being at the fundamental level. Mentally, emotionally, and physically, we are the same. At the physical level, there are little differences, like the size of nose. My nose is considered a big nose. I don't think it's a big nose. So that's very important. We must recognize each other as human beings—no differences. Then, on the secondary level—yes, there are different faiths, different colors, different nationalities. I think, today the problem we are facing is that we emphasize too much on the importance of the secondary level, forgetting that at the fundamental level we are the same human being.

And then also, in today's reality, we must think about all of humanity. I think when we face some problem, we should deal with them with the sense that we are all the same human being. My interest is related with their interest, their interest is related with mine. I always consider I am just one of the nearly now seven billion human beings—I'm a part of the humanity. So my own happy future entirely depends upon rest of the humanity. No matter if one single person is powerful or very rich—he is still part of humanity. If humanity is happy, peaceful and more compassionate, then everybody gets the benefit. And now, in the modern economy, there is no real boundary—no religious boundary.

So that's the reality. The time has come to think for the entire humanity and we must talk on the level of human beings. So when you see me thinking, through my expression, you may to some extent read my mind. Now, for example, everybody has the sense of self—the "I." But nobody pinpoints what that "I" is. Nobody knows. For thousands of years, different traditions have given different explanations about the self, but it is still not very clear. But, anyway, everyone has a sense of self, and with that, the feelings of pain and pleasure. And, by nature, everyone wants happiness, pleasure, and joyfulness. Even animals have the same feelings and the same sort of desire. And since we do not want the experience of pain, we want to overcome problems. That's the basis of the concept of human rights. Everyone has the right to overcome problems and suffering.

The ultimate source of peace of mind and happiness at the mental level is within your self—it is not in money, power, or status. Some of my friends may be billionaires, very rich, but at the personal level they are very unhappy. If you depend on money, it fails to bring inner peace. And also those people who are very powerful, I think that deep inside, they have a lot of anxiety, stress, fear, and distrust. So, material value will not bring real inner joyfulness or peace. Affection or warm-heartedness is what really brings inner strength and self-confidence, and reduces fear and increases friendship and trust. Trust brings friendship. We are social animals—genuine cooperation based on mutual trust is very necessary.

So therefore, once you have a more compassionate mind and warm-heartedness, the whole atmosphere becomes more positive and friendly. Through that way, they say, when you look ahead, you feel, oh, there's my friend; look at this side, there's another friend; look at that side, that person is also your friend. If you keep fear, distrust, and make yourself a little distant from the others, then when another person looks at you, he sees suspicion, distrust, and more caution. As a result, deep inside, you will have a lonely feeling. From that, blood pressure problems and too much stress—all these happen.

On one occasion, in New York, at Columbia University, I had a conference with medical scientists. One medical scientist mentioned in his presentation that people who often express in terms of "I, I, I, my, my" have a greater chance or risk of heart attack. (*Laughs*) He didn't explain why, but I felt it is quite true. As I mentioned earlier, deep inside, these people have fear and distrust; and if you always remain distant from the rest of the people, that brings loneliness. Then it becomes difficult to communicate with other human beings. Ultimately you are a social animal—you are part of the community and you have to deal with others. But because of your own inner weakness, you isolate yourself from them. How can a person like that be happy? So there will be more worry and stress. Once one develops a greater sense of concern for the well-being of other brothers and sisters, an inner door automatically opens and it becomes very easy to communicate with other people. Irrespective of whether one is a believer or nonbeliever, this quality or potential we already have from birth.

Firstly, everybody comes from their mother. Sometimes you see, in India, there are stories about some very great person or saint who was born from a lotus. I jokingly tell people, so such people may have more compassionate attitudes toward the lotus than toward human beings. Fortunately, we were born from our mothers. So as soon as we're born, by a biological factor, on both sides—mother and child—there is an instant and immense feeling of closeness and trust. From the mother's side, that strong emotion of loving kindness or affection brings the energy in order to protect and take care of the child.

This is a biological factor. It does not come from religious faith—no constitution, no police force. The human mother is just like the female cat, dog, or bird—she has a tremendous affection or sense of concern for her offspring. So, biologically, we're equipped with that kind of affection. Any person or any animal who appreciates another's affection also has the potential to show affection to another. Because we were born in that way, we grow up under each other's tremendous affection and care. Then, furthermore, some scientists say that too much anger or fear is actually eating into our immune systems. A more compassionate mind is very helpful to sustain our immune systems. Therefore, in our very blood, there is some kind of seed of affection. With a more compassionate mind, our physical state goes very well. An irritated mind does not go well with the body component. So you can say that basic human nature is more positive and compassionate.

And after all, we are social animals. Even other animals also have limited altruism, because of the need for survival. In the case of human beings, because of their intelligence, their altruistic minds can extend and expand. The compassion, which comes from the biological factor, should be expanded using human intelligence—thinking and the investigation of pros and cons—and then you get conviction and awareness. Warm-heartedness is so important for the society, for the family, and for the individual. If the individual has a more compassionate mind, the individual gets best preserved.

When I'm passing through a street, in my usual sort of way, I always smile. Sometimes the people who're a little bit reserved—and especially some young girls—I think they get a little suspicious when I smile at them. Instead of receiving happiness, they look rather: "Oh, why is this person smiling at me?" So that means, when I smile at another person as a human brother or sister, I feel happy; but my compassionate attitude does not necessarily bring happiness to the other person. It brings them more suspicion and worry. So, as result of the practice of compassion, the first benefit goes to oneself.

I want to make this clear—sometimes people feel that the practice of compassion is something good for other people, but not necessarily for oneself. That's totally mistaken. From our birth, we're already equipped with this potential. Yes, this biological factor of affection exists as a seed. Then we must use human intellect to expand it.

So there are two levels. The first is the level of affection or compassion, which is mainly a biological factor. That's very limited, and also oriented to the other's attitude. That kind of affection goes only toward your friend, or toward the people who show you a positive attitude. The second level of compassion is achieved through training and using our intelligence. As I mentioned earlier, through a judgment of pros and cons, you build conviction. Extremely self-centered attitude is self-destructive. Think more of the other—that really brings inner strength. These convictions deliberately extend your sense of concern and well-being not only toward a friend but also neutral people, and then finally, even toward your enemy or troublemakers. Once you have a genuine sense of concern, which reaches even toward your enemy, then that compassion is genuine and trained. It is unbiased, limitless, and infinite. We can only achieve that level because of this marvellous human intelligence.

One example is of one Tibetan monk I know very well. Since 1959, he spent about eighteen or nineteen years in a Chinese gulag. In the early 1980s, he found the opportunity to come to India and join his previous monastery. I just talked to him about his experience of those eighteen or nineteen years. He told me, during that period, on a few occasions he faced some danger to his life. I asked him, what kind of danger? He told me it was the danger of forgetting compassion, or losing compassion toward his perpetrators, like those Chinese guards. Such a person really practices infinite compassion and is mentally very peaceful and calm.

On one occasion, I simply mentioned the experiences of that monk to a group of scientists. Then, they wanted to test some of these people. After these observations, the scientists found that despite passing through very difficult periods and having very difficult life, this monk's mental state was very peaceful. Usually, people who pass through this kind of experience end up with trauma. But these scientists found, after their interviews and tests, that he had a very peaceful mind. As a result, this particular person, who is now ninety-three or ninety-four, is still physically okay. So I think mental attitude is very important for our health.

About two or three years ago, I had undergone surgery. My gallbladder was removed. Since then, I jokingly telling people— you see my face, which is the same; but in reality, one important organ of the human body is missing from me; so my body is not a complete human body. (*Laughs*) Anyway, usually they say that sort of a surgery takes only fifteen or twenty minutes; but in my case, it took three hours, because of various complications. But then, within six days, within one week, I had completely recovered. The doctor was surprised. Although the surgery itself was quite complicated, the recovery was unusually fast. So that's my own experience.

While I lay down on the surgery table, and afterward during my few days at the hospital, I felt okay. I did not have much anxiety or any other problem. Within a few days, I became very good friends with the nurses and the physicians. I joked with them and teased them. Some of the physicians told me afterward that since our meeting, their whole lives had changed. One physician's wife told me—the physician himself didn't tell me—"My husband used to be a little difficult before. But since that surgery, he has become much gentler."

So, practice compassion because it really benefits not only one-self but creates a kind of positive atmosphere. Of course, I'm not only saying these things from my position as someone special. We all have the same potential—the same intelligence. The only thing is that we have to train it right from childhood. Through training and study, we pay more attention to our inner values. The only necessity is to pay more attention to your inner value—then you will get more experience.

Usually, I listen to BBC a lot. They always talk about money, the economy and politics. And look at the general attitude of people! Unless there is something you can see—or listen to, like music—some people feel really bored. So, all day, they watch television and listen to music. This is, I feel, one indication that we are lacking the experience of inner value, of looking inward and simply thinking about our inner mind. Through that way, we could claim more self-confidence and inner peace. You know, without seeing or hearing, by simply thinking, you get immense peace.

That way, traditionally, people who remain in solitude for years and years—because they have the technique—already know how to bring inner peace through looking inward. Actually, there are two categories of happiness and pain. One depends heavily on sensorial consciousness and experiences—looking at nice things or hearing nice things gives you inner satisfaction. But that kind of satisfaction entirely depends on external means and external things.

The other level of pain and satisfaction does not depend on sensorial experience. Now, for example, when you remember about some past experience, you feel joyfulness or pain. That's the mental level. So between these two—mental-level experiences and physical- or sensorial-level experiences—the mental level is more superior. I think we can discover that mental happiness can subdue physical pain, but mental pain cannot be subdued by physical comfort.

Makes sense? What do you think? Okay? So the mental level is superior, more important and more powerful than the sensory level. Now, modern education in modern society, I think, puts too much emphasis on the sensorial-level experience. I want to share this thought, whose time I think has come now. For at least three or four thousand years, we human beings depended completely on prayer in order to get more happiness or peace of mind. Then, over the last two centuries, science and technology have developed—so the things that we wanted were brought to us immediately through technology. So generally we paid more attention to science and technology rather than to prayer.

Last year, in one Indian state, the state government constructed one Buddhist temple. So the chief minister invited me to the opening ceremony. Then the chief minister—the head of the state government—mentioned in his speech that due to the Buddha's blessing, his state would rapidly prosper. Then it was my turn to speak, and I know him very well, so I expressed, "If your state could rapidly prosper due to the Buddha's blessing, then your state should have developed much earlier; because the Buddha's blessings have been already there for the last 2,500 years. But the Buddha's blessings entirely depend on the work of an able chief minister."

So, it is action that really makes change happen; prayer will not change anything. Therefore, the people's interest in science and technology was natural. As I mentioned earlier, the reports on channels like BBC always talk money. In the later part of the twentieth century, there were two important factors—the first involved those really rich people, who make an affluent, materialistic sort of society. Now, they began to feel that material value alone was not sufficient. Something was lacking, like those few examples I've already mentioned. The other thing was that in science, the research work about neurons in the human brain reached a very deep and sophisticated level. Then they began to develop interest about emotion and the mind. So, we human beings have not only this body but there is also emotion.

Material value provides comfort for the physical level of being, but not for the emotional level. Therefore, now, more and more well-known and well-respected scientists carry out investigations about our emotions, and how to tackle them. So, in the later part of the twentieth century, there began a genuine interest about our inner value. At the same time, in the education system—naturally thousands of years old in the European continent—separate educational institutions started. Before this time, the church took the responsibility to teach people moral ethics. It took responsibility for the family also, to some extent. But that time has now passed, and the influence of the church and the family institution has also declined a little. So the independent educational institution alone should carry the moral responsibility of educating the people about both intellectual subjects and moral ethics or warm-heartedness.

You see, there are a lot of people now who conduct serious research about how to implement some moral ethics and education of warm-heartedness in the modern educational curriculum. We, the people, through our own experiences, are now becoming more mature. So we not only pay attention to material value but also to the internal value. Now here, in that respect, various religious traditions have their own special rules. In the philosophical field, there are basically two categories—theistic religion and non-theistic religion. There are big differences between them. But all teachings and all faiths emphasize the importance of love, compassion, forgiveness, tolerance, self-discipline, and contentment. I have a lot of friends among Christians, Muslims, Hindus, and Jews—genuine practitioners. So we have the same practice, the same potential to transform a human being, and to turn a negative mind into a more positive mind.

When we talk about inner value or moral ethics, various religious traditions have various special rules. Now here, I want to share one thing—your individual religious belief or faith is very important; but you must make a distinction in faith between "one truth, one religion" and several truths and several religions. In terms of the individual, the idea of "one truth, one religion" is very relevant. But in the terms of the society, several truths and several religions are very relevant. So, now how to overcome this contradiction?

One time, in Argentina, I had a meeting with some scientists and religious leaders. One person, he mentioned that he was a physicist, but he believed he should not develop attachment toward his own scientific field. I think that's very great. I'm a Buddhist, but I should not develop attachment toward Buddhism; because you see, if you have too much attachment toward your own faith, then your mind becomes biased. Then you can't see the value of other traditions. You must be faithful toward your own tradition, but you should also have an open mind about others' traditions. You should look at other traditions openly and objectively, and then you will be able to see the value. Nowadays, in the name of religion, there is sometimes division and conflict. That's not because something is wrong with religion, but it's because the practitioner who follows the religion is trapped in attachment.

Religion and harmony are my lifelong commitments and I'm very happy to see different spiritual brothers and sisters here.

So we, in spite of our different philosophies and traditions, we are all practitioners of the same warm-heartedness. So please, take up a more effective role regarding the promotion of inner values. Among nearly seven billion human beings, I think it's very difficult for everyone to become a religious believer. That is also a fact. Here in Ireland, the majority of people, of course, are Catholics, isn't it? But they could also be nonbelievers. So I would like to say to believers, if you follow your religion sincerely and seriously, it has all the potential to provide you with inner peace. But then there are also the nonbelievers, who are not at all serious about religion.

Now, I think there are three ways to promote inner values. Number one—theistic religion; believe in God, totally submit to that God. That kind of faith reduces an extremely self-centered attitude. It is very useful. I first call on the theistic religious way to promote these inner values. Secondly, non-theistic religions—like Buddhism, Jainism, and some other ancient Indian traditions. The believers of these believe in law of causality, which is also a way to promote these inner values. Then, there is a third one, which I usually call the secular way. Here I must make it clear that when I use the word secularism, it does not mean I disrespect all religions, but rather that I respect all religions. According to the Indian concept, secularism means respect for all religions—no preference to this religion or that, because all are equal. And we must also respect the nonbeliever. We must believe that we are the same human being and talk about basic human values. I think that is important. Otherwise, there are people who have no interest in religion. It's wrong to assume that they have also no interest in compassion, because they feel that these are religious matters. That's totally wrong. Whether you accept religion or not, that is up to the individual, but to pay more attention to these inner values is in your own interest.

Sometimes I jokingly tell people, "We are biologically selfish. People are selfish. Because of the selfish feeling, we survived. But that selfish feeling should be wise-selfish rather than foolish-selfish. Taking care of the other's well-being is the best way to achieve your own happiness and a successful life. Out of selfishness, if you only think of yourself and have an extremely self-centered attitude, you will get sugar problems, blood pressure problems, and stress, and eventually get a heart attack." (*Laughs*)

So, of my two lifelong commitments, the first is the promotion of human values, and the second is the promotion of religious harmony. I really appreciate your coming here. Thank you very much. Of the points I mentioned, if you feel an interest in some, then you must yourself experiment and investigate. And then if you feel it is something worthwhile to think about, you must carry out these things in your daily life. If you feel these points are not of much relevance to your life, then forget them—no problem. Thank you!

2
COMPASSION

Budapest, 2010

I'm very happy to be with you, to share some of my views, and also maybe some experiences. We forget our fundamental level of sameness. So now here, when I meet people, I get the feeling that we are the same human being—I'm just talking to another brother or sister, there is no barrier. Of course, the language barrier is there; but my smile, or other physical language, is beyond this language barrier. So, usually my public talks are in two parts—in the first part, I speak about something to you, and then the later part is for questions and answers. I feel there's a mutual benefit in the questions and answers—you get certain points in which you have some personal interest; and through the question, I can understand your current main concern. Sometimes, some unexpected points are raised, so that also, for me, becomes something educational and helpful.

I often use the words "nonbeliever" and "secular ethics," so this session is on that subject. Secular ethics are important because firstly, a large portion of nearly seven billion human beings, in the true sense, are not very serious about religion. So, essentially, these are a type of nonbelievers. These nonbelievers are also human beings and have every right to be happy. We have to take a serious concern in the wants of the nonbeliever. Then comes the subject of secularism itself. As I briefly mentioned yesterday, many of my friends are Christian or Muslim. They're rather reluctant to use the word "secularism," because they have the understanding that secularism means rejection or disrespect of religion.

I think that if people used the word "secular" in the context of the French revolution or the Bolshevik revolution, that would have some meaning against the religious institution—that's okay. In those periods, the religious institution had become the basis of the power of the elite ruling class. Even the Tsar—the Russian king—created an impression that he had special rights in the name of religion, because of God's blessings. And then, these religious institutions themselves were sometimes corrupted. It's worthwhile to be against corrupt religious institutions but that does not mean secularism is genuinely considered anti-religion—only anti the religious institution. According to Indian tradition, secularism does not at all disrespect religion. The constitution of modern India is itself based on secularism. That's not at all out of a sense of disrespect for religion but rather out of respect for all religions—no preference to this religion or that religion. As far as the state is concerned, there is respect for all religions. That's the meaning of secularism.

Sometime back, I met a former Indian deputy prime minister, Mr. Advani. He himself is a religious person, and on one occasion he talked to me about a big interview with him about India's successful democracy on a Canadian television channel. And he told me, he explained in that television interview that the one factor of successful democracy in India is a thousand years old: "India has the habit or tradition of respecting the views of the opposition."

He gave me the example of one school of thought, of Charvaka—nihilism—even before Buddha. According to this, there is no next life, no God, no spirituality, nothing; just this life, so you yourself enjoy as much as you can. So that is the view of Charvaka. Advani told the interviewer that the people who held this view were called nihilists. The rest of India's spiritual tradition criticized and condemned this view; but the people who held this view were also referred to as rishis. Rishi means "sage." So that means that even if you criticize or condemn a philosophical belief, give respect to the persons. That's India's thousand-year-old tradition.

Therefore, look today at India—I think it is the only country where all the world's major religions live together with mutual respect. Of course, in some pockets here and there, some Hindus burn some Christian missionaries, or a Hindu beats up a Muslim, or a Muslim beats up a Hindu. That's okay—that only happens in some pockets here and there. I think that in around one billion human beings, some mischievous people would always be there.

But, considering the larger picture, India is the only country where, besides home-grown religions—like Hinduism, Buddhism, Jainism, and later Sikhism—other religions have also found a peaceful place. Zoroastrianism came from Iran I think thousands of years ago, and found shelter in India. Now they have settled very well. Many public figures, both in the business field and the military, are now Parsi. There are the likes of Tata. Although they are small population, they enjoy equally. Jews, Muslims, Christians—all of the world's major religious traditions have existed in India for a thousand years together. This could only happen, I think, because of the secular attitudes, the respect to all religions. So when I speak about including the nonbeliever, I mean that just like they referred to the ancient nonbeliever as a sage, the modern nonbeliever also has much respect in India. When I say "secularism," I mean it according to the Indian concept.

Now, what are secular ethics? I consider the basic human good qualities have mainly to do with biological factors, and not with the influence of religion. This is true also of certain things that provide us with joyfulness. Like security, the removal of fear—that's a human value and part of secular moral ethics. What is human affection? The time when we were born, our lives entirely depended on our mothers' care. We survived on our mothers' milk. That kind of tireless effort comes from a mother's affection. So the physical effort is from the mother, and every physical action must come from some motivation. So the mother's tireless action of caring for her own child is motivated by affection. This is not only the case with humans. Look at dogs, cats, horses—all these mammals—and also birds.

I know that some small birds, when their eggs hatch, in the beginning the young birds" feathers are too weak to fly. So the mother bird tirelessly flies—comes and goes, comes and goes—collecting food for her children. That energy is brought by affection for her children. It's got nothing to do with religion—it is a biological factor. When someone smiles at us with sincere motivation, we feel happy. That feeling removes fear. So affection brings comfort. These are biological qualities; we already possess these.

When a child is born, it has no idea who any person is, no idea of the mother, but emotionally, because of the biological factor, it totally relies on that person. As long as the mother physically touches that child, the child feels safe and very happy. If it is separated from the mother, it feels unsafe and insecure. Animals are also like that. Once I noticed some puppies, very small at the time, their eyes not yet opened. They made a little sound and tried to seek their mothers'—what is it?— that small thing, from which milk comes? (*Audience laughs*) You see, the kitten or the puppy whose eyelids have still not opened, but it has the ability make its way to that small thing. And as soon as it reaches its mouth, it's very happy and peaceful. That's the proof of the tremendous affection between the mother and the child. I think the experience we receive at that time—when we are ourselves helpless and ignorant but survive because of our mothers' care and affection—really reaches deep in our blood.

It remains like that all our life—whenever we receive affection from others, we feel happy. Even at the time of death, people know they will no longer remain together—one is dying, the other will remain, so now there can be no more friendship, no more use—but still, the dying person is emotionally much happier when surrounded by good friends who are really showing affection to him or her. That's the nature of human life.

This very body of the person, when it is surrounded by affectionate persons, also becomes healthier and stronger. Some medical doctors and scientists performed a particular experiment. They took two guinea pigs, both wounded with the same injury. They put one injured guinea pig with another healthy one, so the injured guinea pig constantly received licks from its friend. The other was kept without a friend or companion, so there was no possibility for it to receive licks. It was found that the guinea pig receiving licks recovered much faster. So that's the result of receiving affection.

Although affection is not physical, only mental, it has a tremendous effect on the body. Some scientists even told me that negative emotions like anger, hatred, and fear can actually eat into our immune systems. On the other hand, affection and genuine friendship are very helpful to sustain our immune system—sometimes they even make it function better. So that's the fact, and now it is also scientifically proven. Scientists also performed another experiment on baby monkeys, where some baby monkeys were allowed to stay with their mothers, and the others were separated from theirs. It was observed that the baby monkeys who were with their mothers always had a playful and happy mood. The ones which were separated from their mothers were almost always frustrated and ready to fight.

Then on one occasion in Washington, at a university, we discussed the relationship between compassion and physical health. According to one physician's experiment, people who often express in words like "I, my, mine, me" have a greater risk of heart attacks. He didn't express the reason. Within that narrow scale, even small problems appear very big and unbearable to you. On the other hand, when you think more out of concern for others' well-being, your mind widens. So with that view, even serious problems will not seem that significant.

There are thousands of people more concerned with their own well-being rather than your well-being. So there the narrow-minded attitude magnifies the small problems, the reaction is very strong and as a result, there is more fear, frustration, anxiety—all

THE DALAI LAMA'S BIG BOOK OF HAPPINESS

this is very bad for our health. Besides, we are social animals, so good relations with the surrounding human companions are very essential. If one has a truly self-centered attitude, you automatically develop suspicion and distrust, and it is very difficult to develop genuine human friendship.

For the people who have some sense of others' well-being, the other is considered something cherishable, so their contact with other people is much easier, much more possible. The result is that there is no fear or anxiety. Trust is based on honesty and being transparent. If you remain in hypocrisy, how can you develop trust? Without trust, how can you develop friendship? If you are rich, because of your money, you may buy some more guests. But that would only get you a superficial smile or a few nice words—deep inside, there would be no respect. Genuine friendship is based on trust. That's basic human nature.

If you think along these lines, you will automatically develop the conviction that in order to get maximum benefit for yourself, you should be honest, compassionate, and not have an extremely self-centered attitude. It's selfish and brings more suffering, more trouble and worry for you. It also spoils your physical condition. We are all born from mothers. Everyone generally experiences one's own mother's milk. Everybody's first experiences are of the mother's kindness and affection. After that, using our common sense and experience, we develop and build conviction. Cultivating a more altruistic attitude is the best way to bring inner peace and good health. Then there are scientific findings. So then these are three ways—personal experiences, common sense and scientific findings—through which we can develop a deeper awareness of the importance of compassion and affection. Through that, we can promote basic values and good qualities.

Aggressiveness and anger are also a part of human nature, but they are wrong. We take these things for granted. Some of these aspects of human nature are supposed to protect us, but in the meantime, they damage our intelligence and ability to see the reality. When anger develops, we can't see the reality because much mental projection is involved. Therefore, even if you want to despise someone or want to harm others, your method should be realistic. Through realistic methods, you get what you want. Any unrealistic method cannot get you to the goal. Without knowing the reality, all our methods become unrealistic methods and fail to get our goals. So, too much aggressiveness, greed, self-centered attitude, fear, and distrust are really very harmful for the normal function of human intelligence. I think I will stop here now.

QUESTIONS

QUESTION: *Your Holiness, in one's life, where is the point until which you should strive to realize your wishes and your desires? And which is the point where you should stop? My question is applicable to every part of our everyday life, like partnership, raising children, the workplace and everything else.*

HIS HOLINESS: That's quite a big question. Of course, for all of the desires or objectives which we want to achieve, firstly we must analyze how much we can achieve them. Then, we should have a realistic approach, so we get more satisfactory results. If our approach is unrealistic or the goal too big, it cannot materialize in any way. So that's important at the beginning.

Then, I think, basically there are two things—our goal for material values and another for internal values, like peace or calmness of mind. Where material values are concerned, there's always a limitation—even if you become a billionaire, your greed may still not be satisfied, you may want more and more, and finally, you will hit a limitation. Anyway, when there's a limitation, you may better practice contentment. There is no limitation to internal value—more effort and practice will continue to yield more result. These good mental qualities always increase because they are not based on the physical.

Any value based on the physical will have a limitation. For example, eyesight has a limitation because it depends on the eye organs and the brain. Mental state is not based on the physical level, so greater the training, more the development. In that field, logically, you should always make the effort and try to improve, because the scope is infinite. Usually we do just the opposite. In the material field, where in any case there's a limitation, we're never content. We always want more and more. But where inner value is concerned, we are content. That is a mistake.

QUESTION: *Your Holiness, what is your opinion about eating meat? The animals that we hunt, kill, and eat also want to live. I wonder what they feel. What is the effect of eating meat on the human intellect and human mind?*

HIS HOLINESS: Vegetarianism is a thousand-year-old tradition, and I think it's something very good. In Tibet, traditionally, of course—in some areas in the Tibetan plateau—there's no vegetable or fruit; and in ancient times, Tibetan life depended entirely on animals, for milk, meat, skin, fur, and things like that. So basically, Tibetans are Buddhist, but are in the meantime non-vegetarian. In my own case, when my age was I think fourteen or fifteen, I changed the official festival menus, which previously involved lots of meat, into vegetarian food. Then after 1965, I tried to become vegetarian. For the next twenty months, I remained vegetarian. But after that my gallbladder problem started, so then, I think around 1967, I again returned to my previous non-vegetarian diet.

Later, all our bigger monastic institutions stopped serving meat and began serving vegetarian food from their common kitchens. The common kitchens of some schools also voluntarily gave up serving meat. And then, at all the Tibetan settlements in India, we decided not to open piggeries, fisheries, and poultry farms. One or two settlement kept some poultry, they said, only for the eggs. Then I asked them, what do you do after the hens stop giving eggs? There were no clear answers. A few hundred hens were just kept even after they stopped giving eggs; feeding them was also expensive. After that, they were distributed to each family, which was also a burden.

So I asked if the poultry farm for eggs was really necessary for economic reasons, really necessary for the settlement. If it was not that important, I requested them to close down the poultry farm. So now, for the last two decades, none of the settlements has had a poultry farm. So that's our own small contribution toward the promotion of vegetarianism. As for the individual, it's up to them.

At the mental level, what is the effect of non-vegetarianism on the mind is difficult to say. I don't know. But then, there is also the matter of ecology. Big beef and other meat farms are also very bad for the ecology. The way they force-feed the animals—trying to make them grow rapidly and unnaturally and become fat—is also very bad for our health. Nowadays, scientists are saying that the so-called organic production is better for our health. Recently, certain illnesses have spread because of beef, pork, and chicken. There are also some reports that the number of fish in some areas have now reduced because of overfishing. I think we should have some limitations, instead of mercilessly producing millions of these animals and then killing them.

And in the meantime, if the entire human race becomes vegetarian, that is also impractical and difficult. But I think it is important to educate human beings that are mercilessly raising these animals and mercilessly selling their meat, without feeling their pain and without respect for their lives; this is certainly wrong. We cannot make rules, but through education, we can improve awareness.

QUESTION: *What are the most important values we should teach our children?*

HIS HOLINESS: This morning, we had some serious lectures on Buddhism and also on meditation, where there were some very young children. I think they are used to maximum freedom—running around here, going there—and at that age, I think they do not consider the importance of social background, or whether one is educated or uneducated. They don't care, so long as they play together, they are smiling. I think that's a very pure state of mind. At this age, they appreciate other's affection and care very much.

Gradually, as they are growing up, these children will get more independent and rely less and less on each other's care. Then, the appreciation of another's affection becomes not as much relevant. At that level, I think we need, through education, to remind them that affection is very important for our lives. And that you should be a more affectionate person, because it's in your own best interest. I think in America, and also Canada, on a number of occasions, there were some serious discussions on the importance of the subjects of love and compassion in modern-day education. Or, in other words, the role of moral ethics in the modern-day education system. I see lots of talks taking place in Quebec and Montreal. There have been special teachers' training on how to introduce moral ethics in a secular education system. They invited me and I also talked. So, there are some people really working, on research, on how to introduce moral ethics on a secular basis in the modern education system.

So eventually, I hope there are some new ideas on the ways to educate children about moral ethics through public and secular-education schools, without touching on religion. And in the meantime, for parents, it is equally important to suggest and advise them not just on subjects like history, but on compassion and affection, through demonstration, not just words. If a parent or teacher is talking about compassion but displaying angry face, it is impossible to bring conviction to the child's mind. So this should be taught through action—genuine loving kindness, real affection. There are curriculums that don't include the subject of moral ethics on a secular basis, but you, as a teacher, may teach your student about these moral ethics and values.

I think, at present, of the many problems we are facing, some are major disasters, beyond our control, but some are actually man-made problems, like the fear of terrorists and conflict in the name of different religious traditions. And also, in some cases, the problem is created on the basis of discrimination. As I mentioned before, fundamentally, we are the same human being. Everyone has the same right to be happy. But due to discrimination, there are unnecessary problems.

I feel really proud that in India's ancient tradition of ahimsa—non-violence—there is a sense of religious harmony. Really, I feel proud that these traditions still remain in India. Meanwhile, there is also the caste system and discrimination on the basis of caste. These traditions are outdated, and we must address them seriously. These problems are man-made—our own creations—and any problem that is our own creation we must have the ability or right to change. I strongly feel like that. I heard that on some island in the Pacific Ocean, the mother is the main person in the community, in the family. So there is female dominance and some special rights for mothers; I think we should learn more from that tradition.

QUESTION: *Your Holiness, if we do believe in incarnation or reincarnation, why are we afraid of overpopulation, if the reason for that is reincarnation? Isn't there a contradiction?*

HIS HOLINESS: No. From the Buddhist viewpoint, and also according to some ancient Indian traditions, the world is limitless. Obviously, you use your common sense. Now, out of the billions of galaxies that are there, only on this planet, only in this solar system—only here—there are human beings. It's difficult to say, but there must be billions of similar planets that can support life. So there must be more life among them. So we are like tourists. We come from some other place, spend some hundred years there, and then again go somewhere. That's how it is from the Buddhist viewpoint, so there is no contradiction.

QUESTION: *Does Your Holiness believe that in your lifetime, in the coming twenty or forty years, the major religions of the world will be able to cooperate and work together toward the realization of one common goal? What is your advice for the average human being about what we can do for such a dialogue?*

His Holiness: Pope John Paul II initiated the Assisi Meeting. This involved not only the leaders of different Christian denominations but also of some Asian religions—Buddhist, Hindu, and Muslim. At the Vatican, I think their documents now use the word "pluralism." So it seems now that worldwide, the concepts of several religions are growing.

One important observation is the concept of one religion, one truth, and the concept of several religions and several truths—these two are apparently contradictory, but both are important. Now, how can we overcome this contradiction? The concept of one truth and one religion, in the terms of one individual, is very important in order to strengthen his faith toward his own religion. But in the terms of a community, in the terms of several people … For example, at this very moment, there are different people of different religions here. So the fact is that several truths, several religions already exist here. So, in the terms of the individual, there is one truth and one religion; in the terms of the community, the concept of several truths and several religions is relevant. There is no contradiction; we have to make a distinction between faith toward one's own religion and respect to all religions. So, no contradictions—this awareness is growing but still, I think we need more effort.

Usually, I have four ideas that I have been practicing and implementing for more than thirty years. Firstly, I meet with scholars from different traditions and academic levels to see what similarities and what differences exist. When we find differences, for example, in philosophy, then I move on to the second step—a dialogue between practitioners about their really deep experiences. That brings deeper understanding of the value and the potential of the other's religion, and it is very useful.

And the third is to look at the big image, like visiting the holy places of different traditions. There was a feeling I had in France at Lourdes, in Portugal at Fatima, and then, of course, at Rome and Jerusalem. Once, after my lecture on the Christian gospel to a Christian group in England, some Christian brothers and sisters who came to India actually came to Bodhgaya. So each morning, the Christian group spent half an hour under the Bodhi tree in silent meditation. It was very useful. One can experience some vibrations from these holy places. One time at Lourdes, in front of the image of Jesus Christ, I felt an immense admiration and appreciation for this holy place, which provides great benefit and inspiration for millions and millions of Christians.

And at Fatima, one morning, we visited one holy place there, which had one small Mary statue. We spent some time in front of Mary's statue in silent meditation. Then, when we were leaving, I turned back to that small statue and I actually saw her smiling. So, I felt some kind of blessing from Mary. Of course, technically, I'm not a follower of Mary or Jesus Christ, but I genuinely respect and admire that tradition. So I think I received some blessing.

And the fourth method is like the Assisi Meeting where the heads of different traditions come together, and speak in the same voice of peace and spirituality. This method of promoting closer understanding of different religious traditions, and most importantly, wider contact, is very essential.

3

COMPASSION AND CIVIC RESPONSIBILITY

Seattle, 2008

I ndeed, I'm very happy and feel great honor to have received this degree and also got an opportunity to talk to young boys and girls. I think you all look very bright in your eyes. One student quite bright *here* also. (*Points to his own head and to a bald student*) I think we two are competing. (*Laughs*) Sorry! So, these young people—you are the basis of our hope. I was born in 1935, just before the Second World War; then came the Korean War, the Vietnam War, and also India's Partition and the civil war in China. The wars continue up to now, in Africa and the Middle East.

I think each individual's life is dearest to him, but there is no value to the preciousness of life. Now I am nearly seventy-three and I observed the last century. Of course, there were many great movements in the fields of science and everything else, but the last century also became the century of war and violence. I think the people who started this violence were certainly there with a hope or a vision. Although they chose a violent method, they were hoping to bring brighter days on this planet, or, at least, to the people who concerned them. But it seems that violence and counter-violence are an endless cycle.

So therefore, you, the new generation of the twenty-first century—you are our hope. You will build this century as a century of peace and tranquility. No more bloodshed. Each individual's dearest self lives happily. Everybody is saying, "Peace, peace" a thousand times, but peace does not come from the sky. Why? Violence and war are our creations, so peace depends on us. We must make a lasting peace. So my generation—we the professors, chancellors, and others who belong to the twentieth century—are ready to say goodbye. (*Waves fingers*) Now is the time to hand it over—all this mess in the world—to you. You have to find the ways and the means to work on this problem.

Firstly, in order to carry out the effective ways and methods to bring peace, you need the willpower to face any conflict without using violence but through dialogue, and face-to-face interaction.

I often tell people that this century should be the century of dialogue. Dialogue is the only way to solve conflict. If we hope for a peaceful world without any conflict, that is unrealistic. I think as long as we human beings, with our intelligence, have the ability of different visions, there will always be different hopes and different ideas. Also with global warming, limitation of major resources, and increase in population, there are bound to be factors for conflict. So peace means that we challenge these conflicts without using force but through peaceful means, through dialogue.

Now in order to carry on dialogue, we need will and determination; and here, determination needs to be based on compassion. That means you simply must respect others' rights and interests, and instinctively refrain from harming others. To ensure that, we need a compassionate heart. Secondly, we need wisdom and a more holistic view of the reality—the full picture. So, although it comes from Buddhism and Buddhist philosophy, the concept of interdependency is something I feel is adaptable to everyone. Everything's interdependent.

Now, in today's world, in the matters of economy and other things, not only individual nations but even continents are mutually interdependent. Under these circumstances, there's hardly a nation or a group of people which is the enemy. They are all a part of ourselves. Therefore, destruction of your enemy or your neighbor is actually destructive to yourself. Taking care of your so-called enemy—who may have different views, different attitudes, and maybe a slightly negative attitude toward you—is also a part of yourself. Your future depends on them. Now, using violence to defeat a neighbor is meaningless. In ancient times, the defeat of your neighbor or your enemy meant victory for you. Today, it means mutual destruction. Therefore, the concept of war is outdated.

So, on the one hand, try to strengthen compassion toward all forms of life. On the other hand, on the basis of the theory of interdependency, develop a holistic view. Combine these two things and I think we can bring genuine, lasting peace to the world. If a person is full of hatred, anger, and fear, then peace is simply lip service. Genuine peace must come from within. Therefore, in order to achieve genuine peace or world peace, first we must start with our individual selves, in our minds, in our emotional worlds. We must aim for tranquility and calm. Of course, disturbances, hatred, anger and too much suspicion are bound to happen, but these should be only at the surface level. Deep inside, we must respect all forms of sentient beings and know that our future depends on them. Combine these two things and, deep inside, you can sustain peace and inner calmness. These destructive emotions are almost impossible to stop, but they should not gain strength. With a deeply compassionate mind and wisdom, you can maintain inner peace.

So through one individual's inner peace, you can create a peaceful family, and then a peaceful community. If eventually we create that kind of a community, then the people in leadership roles—the politicians, the civil servants, the military personnel or anyone who comes from the community—will be different. That's the way to bring in a genuine peaceful world, or lasting world peace.

As far as education is concerned, you are the experts. Particularly, all these wonderful professors, of course, are fully equipped as far as knowledge is concerned. I feel too shy to speak in front of these big scholars. However, the factor that gives me a little courage to express my opinion is modern education. I may be wrong, but it seems to me that modern education is mainly focusing on external or material development. I agree we can't blame that, because now the educational institution alone has the responsibility to take care of both intellectual education and moral ethics.

As far as moral ethics is concerned, there are different views. One view is that moral ethics must be based on religious faith; another view is this is not necessarily so. Moral ethics can be secular ethics and should be universal. So therefore, with earnest respect, professors as well as students, please pay sufficient attention to inner values, especially to that of warm-heartedness. That much I wanted to share with you.

Now, what else I should say?—I don't know. (*Laughs*) The other day, I mentioned something that I do not think is wrong to repeat. In order to develop inner peace, you need some kind of inner disarmament. As I mentioned earlier, complete elimination of destructive emotions is impossible. But we can weaken these, so negative emotion can come, but cannot disturb, because of positive inner strength. That is what I call inner disarmament.

Anger and hatred may bring extra energy. A scientist told me that biologically, when anger develops, blood rushes into your hand, which means it is ready to hit. Similarly, when fear develops, blood goes to the legs, which indicates that you must now run away. These two are very important emotions for survival and as these emotions develop, biological changes take place accordingly. I think, at a limited level, anger is good—for defense. But as we grow up, sometimes the anger and the hatred grow with us. Our human intelligence, instead of expanding compassion, expands our hatred. That is wrong.

Our intelligence must help in growing compassion, and should not be at the disposal of hatred. Now there is something Buddhists call analytical meditation—simply to analyze and calculate the value of anger and hatred. Anger and hatred are supposed to harm others, but in reality, as soon as anger and hatred develop, they immediately destroy your own peace of mind. And in the process you lose your sleep, digestion, appetite and then, eventually, you become physically weak. As a result of the constant anger and hatred, the best part of your brain, which can judge, is also reduced and weakened. If you are in a state where you are reduced both mentally and physically, it would give advantage to your enemy.

If you have some conflict and constantly feel anger toward your neighbor, eventually you will suffer. When you suffer, maybe your neighbor has his moment of victory. Instead of that, you must remain calm. If your neighbor is unjust toward you, it is necessary and appropriate to put up a counter-measure, but without anger or hatred. Analyze the situation and take your effective counter-measure with a smile. That is more effective, isn't it? So hatred is almost of no use. If you think along these lines, you will realize that hatred is something that deserves to be thrown into the waste-paper basket.

A little anger is okay when you are young—just like any other animal—for immediate self-defense. But as a grown-up, you must think very carefully—what use is that anger? On the other hand, there is compassion. Because we are grown-ups, with the help of our intelligence, we can expand our limited compassion to infinite compassion. If your compassion is unbiased, it can also reach out to your enemy. Once that kind of mental ability is achieved, you can certainly keep a peaceful mind all the time. Even when you confront some difficult situation, you will still have peace of mind. So that's inner disarmament.

Through that way, external disarmament will gradually come. That is also necessary. Since the concept of war is outdated, weapons are now of no use. Perhaps a small, limited mobile force will be necessary, as there will always be some mischievous people. Now some countries, I remember, have no army. In those countries, comparatively, the economy, education, and health are much better, because all the resources are used for that; while their neighboring countries' resources are spent buying weapons, ammunition, and mercenaries. So we should hope and pray toward the eventual aim of a demilitarized world. Of course, this cannot happen overnight. Now for that, firstly, I think we must check arms trade. Some Nobel laureate has already carried out some initiative regarding this. That's wonderful, that's very good. It is also worthwhile to explore the possibility of a Franco-German unified force. Hopefully, in the European continent, all the member states of the European Union will create a unified force—like their unified currency, eventually they must have a unified force.

These are actually beyond my business, but as a sort of freedom of speech and thought, I often express these things. I think it's a good idea to have a dream, so some positive changes may happen. Then, gradually, there will be a global-level army. If something like that happens, I think it will be for the best. So I take the opportunity to share some of my dreams, for an energetic, long, bright future for these young students. Please keep that in your mind. Firstly, you should be a more peaceful person. Then, extend your experience and your views—your right views and right behavior. Like throwing a stone into pond, it creates a ripple effect.

So, thank you, that's all—thank you.

QUESTIONS

QUESTION: *What is the simplest act of compassion with the most positive effect?*

HIS HOLINESS: Simplest? Most positive effect? I don't know. I think one must pay more attention to our inner worlds. That means a world of psychology, emotions, and thoughts. Although in the ancient times these things started out as part of religion and philosophy, usually I divide them into three paths.

In Buddhism, I divide them into Buddhist science, Buddhist philosophy, and Buddhist religion. Buddhist philosophy, to some extent, and certainly Buddhist religion, are only for Buddhists, and have nothing to do with other people. But Buddhist science is something common. Now in the West, the scientists who are working on the human brain, neurons, and emotion are beginning to look at the more detailed information from the ancient Indian tradition. So, I think it's useful. To get some information, experiment by yourself. So that much I can say— the rest I don't know.

QUESTION: *What is the ultimate vision that you have for the whole world, which you feel will be realistically achievable in the next few decades?*

HIS HOLINESS: I think that within this century itself, if we make the effort, mainly through education, I think a more friendly, peaceful, and compassionate world can be achieved. The demilitarized world—I don't know. But certainly, the rate of conflict can go down. That kind of better world is very possible, realistically speaking.

Oh, I want to add one thing. In the material world, one problem is the gap between the rich and the poor. This is true not only at the global level but also at a national level. Look at the USA, where the number of billionaires is increasing, but the poorer section of the people still remain poor. I think Singapore may be better—almost like a city-state, isn't it? I think this gap may be less there, I don't know. Otherwise, in India, now unfortunately in China also, the gap between the rich and the poor is rapidly increasing. This is not only morally wrong, but is also a source of practical problems. I think we should seriously address this problem. That's very important.

So this is where the role of compassion becomes important—the richer family or society should take serious concern in the needs of the poorer sectors of the world. Within the nation as well, the wealthier people should give education, training, give skills or equipment to the poor and should not look down upon them; they must help them attain self-confidence.

I don't think anyone is born inferior or superior. Eventually, these divisions are our creations. One time, when I was in South Africa, I visited a black family, where a member of the family was a teacher. And this was just after the change, with South Africa having become a democratic country. So I told the family, "Your constitution has now changed—everybody is equal, there are no longer any racial divisions or discriminations—but mentally or emotionally it will still take time to adjust." Then I expressed, "Now the black community must take the opportunity fully, and realize it through education, training, and self-confidence." And then that teacher told me, "Our brains are inferior. We cannot match the white people."

At that moment I felt very sad. That's the source of the problem now. I told this man, "Absolutely wrong. From birth, our brains are the same. The difference in color is just superficial. Basically we are the same human being—same potential, same capacity." I gave him the example of the Tibetan situation. I told him that if everyone got the same opportunities, we could prove that we were the same, we were equal. I had a long discussion with him. Then finally, with long sighs, whispering to me, the man was convinced that we were same. That moment, I felt some kind of tremendous relief—at least one person's mental attitude was changed now! Therefore, the richer or more successful section of the human population should pay more attention and show a genuine sense of concern for the human brothers and sisters on the other side, until the other side also eventually gains self-confidence. In the meantime, the rich should provide them with education, healthcare, and money. Only then would the weaker section of the population get rid of the trends of frustration and violence, and work hard, study hard—that's the way of bridging this gap. So I think one of the responsibilities of today's youth is to do something serious about this gap. That much I wanted to share.

QUESTION: *How do we show compassion to someone who has been harming other people?*

HIS HOLINESS: As I mentioned before, biased compassion and unbiased compassion are two things. Biased compassion is generally a biological product. It comes to us from birth. Then, with the help of our intelligence and knowledge—a fuller knowledge of long-term and short-term consequences—our compassion becomes unbiased. That kind of compassion, born out of wisdom or knowledge, can extend toward your enemy. There are reasons for this. The person who creates harm on another does it out of negative emotion. So there's a sort of a reason to feel concerned about him.

Then, of course, there are two things—the victim's side and the perpetrator's side. In the long term, there is more reason to take concern for the perpetrator, because, firstly, according to theistic religion, he is acting against God's wish and will have to face negative consequences. The non-theistic religious view is that the perpetrator of harm accumulates negative karma, so sooner or later, again, he has to face negative consequences. So there is more reason to feel concern for the perpetrator. On the other hand, since the victim has already suffered, from the theistic viewpoint, God will now be willing to take greater care of him; and from the non-theistic viewpoint, he has already closed a chapter of karmic balancing from the past. Does this make sense? Even from the secular viewpoint, the wrong-doing person—the perpetrator of harm, the murderer, the thief, the liar, the sexual abuser—will have to face the consequences of the law. So there's a reason to feel concern for him. And on that basis, extend him your sense of compassion.

QUESTION: *Do you consider the environment to be a luxury for the rich, and what can we do to maintain a balance between our compassion for other people and our planet?*

HIS HOLINESS: The environment issue, for me, is a new subject and understanding. When we were in Tibet, the climate was dry and cold, the population was small, all water could be drunk—there was no problem. So we had no idea about polluted water. So eventually, as a result of a number of meetings with scientists and experts about ecology, I noticed how this is a very serious issue. This planet of six billion human beings is the only home for all those six billion. The moon looks nice against the dark night—there are a lot of poems about the moon—but if we lost our own home and tried to settle on the moon, it would be hopeless. I think this blue planet is the only home for human beings and other sentient beings.

I think global warming may be due to the sun and the position of our planet according to the sun—that's beyond our control. I think five billion years ago, when this planet was gradually forming, the situation was not like that. So in the future, after few more billions of years, our sun will also disappear. So these things are a different question. But to some extent, due to our own error, we cause a great deal of global warming. This is a very serious issue now. Another factor is the bloodshed which I mentioned.

But environmental degradation is invisible. Without much notice, it is affecting our breathing, our lungs, our eyes, which maybe we don't notice until too late. Therefore, this is more serious. We have to pay much more attention to it. Then this is not a matter of justice that we can merely talk about—this is a matter of practice. Therefore, thinking about the environment should be part of our daily lives. My own little silly contribution toward that, I think now for the last few decades, is that I never use a bathtub, only a shower. Even so, taking this shower every day—once in the morning and once in the evening—is a big luxury. So acting responsibly toward the shortage of water or electricity, I think, should be part of our daily lives.

Now, how can this concern be connected to compassion? In the responsibility to save the environment, individual effort may not seem very significant. But if one person practices the concern—and then ten people, a hundred people, a thousand people—they eventually make a difference. So the initiative must come from the individual. I usually call this a sense of "global responsibility"—a sense of the well-being of six billion human beings. So here is the connection with compassion. It comes from both a sense of concern for the other, and a sense of concern for oneself.

Actually, one must first love oneself. That is very essential. So first, take the maximum care of yourself; then for your own benefit, extend love to others.

QUESTION: *As HIV continues to devastate populations in Africa, what do you think we can do to get people interested in it and show the compassion and love necessary to turn this disease around?*

HIS HOLINESS: Firstly, of course, I think there is already some research being done about HIV. Millions of dollars are being spent. I think this should continue, and will hopefully bring us some results. The next step of awareness is education. There are some cases where HIV may spread through blood transfusion; but in most cases it spreads through sexual contact, doesn't it? So maybe more rubber should be made available. (*Laughs*) There's another thing—I think the community should not reject or look down upon these patients.

QUESTION: *Some people tend to be less compassionate by nature. Is there a way to cultivate compassion for people in their lives?*

HIS HOLINESS: At the beginning of our lives—in early childhood—I don't think there is much difference. But after birth, from the very first day and through the weeks and months, different environments and conditions turn us into different kinds of people. That's why it is extremely important to provide a young child with maximum affection from the parents; and allow the mother—particularly the mother—to spend more time with the child. And instead of any other milk, I feel the mother's own milk is the best for the child.

Patience is also a really important matter. Time is also a factor. Turning something from good to bad is quite easy. But changing something from bad to good takes a longer time and needs more effort, so naturally it also needs more patience. The other day, on my flight from Tokyo to Seattle, there was a couple with two children. At the beginning they seemed very nice. I gave some candies to the young boy—I think one of them was a boy, and the other was a girl. Then, the whole night the older child slept nicely; but the younger child kept shouting, crying, and moving about. Then eventually the father went silent, and then fell asleep. But the mother spent the whole night taking care of that child. At the time I felt, if I were in that position, I may not have the sufficient patience. Thank you.

QUESTION: *With all the discontent, crime, racism, and hate, what can we, as people, do to incorporate compassion, to make a difference in the lives of others and our society?*

HIS HOLINESS: Like any other problem, we need long-term solutions and short-term solutions. As for long-term solutions, as I have already mentioned, we should use education to promote and make people aware of their inner value. That is the only way in the long term. A peaceful society cannot be brought about by regulation, order, or bullying—that's difficult. It can only come true if individuals volunteer their initiative. That's why we need the awareness of this inner value.

The short term, on the other hand, I don't know. I have no particular experience. Perhaps it can be done by making some relevant connection. When I visited Northern Ireland, I saw victims of the clash between two religious groups. I have been to the country two or three times. On one occasion, I was invited to visit a group of victims. When I entered that room, everybody's face was tense and unsmiling, as if ready to fight. The atmosphere, on both sides, was full of hatred. Then we sat down and talked. At first, I listened to their experiences. All of it was a very horrible sort of experience. Then, I tried to make the atmosphere a little calm by smiling, sharing a few jokes, things like that. Eventually, they warmed up to me a little, and we gradually had a serious exchange.

When I went to Northern Ireland the next time, after one or two years, I visited these victims a second time, and there was a big difference! Right from the beginning, the victims began to smile. There was a man among them whom I describe as my hero. I think his age was thirteen or fourteen when a rubber bullet hit him here (*points between his eyebrows*), and instantly, his eyesight was gone. Of course, because of the pain, at that moment, the boy lost consciousness. When his consciousness returned, he was already blind. But there was no anger or hatred in him—just the regret that he could no longer see his mother's face, he told me. As a result, when I first met this group of victims, this blind man was still calm and had a smile on his face. When I met him again on my second visit, he already had a beautiful wife and two children—two very beautiful girls.

So mental attitude really makes a big difference in your life. Of victims of the same atrocity, some keep anger and hatred for the rest of their lives, and their years are tense and difficult. This boy, right from the beginning, had no anger or hatred. Therefore his life—although he has no eyesight—is very happy there. So perhaps this story, and sharing and telling these stories, if it's some really troubled area, I think it worthwhile to invite my hero, I think it's really wonderful, I think the outside world is not much aware of this person. So I think just make friendship, first from inside reach out. Then gradually their tremendous frustration reduces, and then we can make more serious discussion, this I feel. I think with better education, better awareness, better intermix, these will gradually change. I feel like that.

QUESTION: *Compassion and civic responsibility are words with broad interpretations and many meanings. Is there a universal definition effective enough to connect people, despite differences in our religion, class, age, and gender?*

HIS HOLINESS: I think civic responsibility means a certain sense of responsibility for the society. The basic human nature is of a social animal. First of all, I don't know the exact meaning of this English term—"civic responsibility." As I already mentioned, unless you have the sense of caring or concern about others' well-being, that kind of responsibility is difficult to have. So clearly this connection.

Now compassion. I think compassion is the sense of concern for others' suffering; I think that part is the same according to all religious traditions. Love and compassion I think are the same. But then with the concept of God, the wisdom side is different. As I mentioned earlier, now there are six billion human beings; we must find a universal way that's on the basis of our common sense, common experience. The affection between mother and child is universal. It is even common to those mammals whose life depends on the mother, dogs, and cats. We are just like them, same pattern. So we human beings, because of our intelligence and now scientific findings, can have a more compassionate mind. The brain functions better, the physical health is also better. I think these are universal. So use these as the basis of explanation of the importance of compassion. That's, I think, the secular way, that's very, very important.

So thank you.

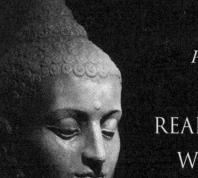

Part Three

REALITY AND
WISDOM

1

ANCIENT WISDOM
AND MODERN THOUGHT

Mumbai, 2011

Indeed, I feel a great honor to speak with you. Particularly at this university, since it is the very famous Bombay University. I always feel very happy meeting with students. I believe the younger generation—whose age is below thirty or even twenty—is really the generation of this century, the generation that can make anew the shape of this world. Time is always moving—no force can stop time. But then, what we can do is to utilize time properly. I think that, at a global level, the generation that belongs to the twenty-first century is the main generation that has the responsibility to create a better world.

In the twentieth century, of course, great achievements were made both in the technological field and in science. However, that century also became a century of bloodshed and violence. And since the Second World War, there is constant fear, particularly in the European countries. Though they are apparently at peace, underneath there is constant fear, something I noticed myself on a visit to West Germany's border area.

All this is part of the same human world, but because of technology, some of us have gained tremendous destructive power. Sometimes I really feel that this marvellous human intelligence is sometimes used for wrong purpose. Anyway, because we learned from such unhappy situations in the past century, now the younger generation must have vision to create a different world. World peace means a world of peace and peace does not come through sky, or through paper; peace must come through inner peace. As I mentioned earlier, sometimes these nuclear weapons act as a deterrent. They may have brought some superficial peace, but only out of fear. That's not genuine peace. Now the question is how to develop inner peace.

Inner peace by medicine? No. Tranquilizers, maybe, but only for a short period. Or drugs? No. Then, can education bring inner peace? Again, not very sure. Some of these real troublemakers—as far as their brains are concerned—are very smart, very educated. But they use their brains in a destructive way. So I am very much keen to meet the younger generation in different parts of the world. When I meet the Indian youth, the Indian public, I have a certain emotional feeling. Actually, since Buddhism reached Tibet, then whole Tibetan civilization has been much enriched and much developed. So the time when Morarji Desai took up the prime ministership, as usual, I wrote a letter of congratulation. And then in his reply, Morarji Babuji mentioned that the Tibetan civilization and the Indian are two branches of one bodhi tree—same root. So I usually describe the Indians as our gurus. We are chelas of the Indian guru. So when I interact with Indians, sometimes I feel I'm talking to you about facts that essentially we learned from you. I feel great honor. And then, Bombay is the heart of India's economy, so very important. So I'm very happy for this opportunity.

Now, as I mentioned earlier, time is always moving. And then, the world—because of global warming, because of population increase and also some political systems—sometimes also causes some problems. And then in the economy, the gap between the rich and poor is also a very serious matter. Unfortunately, in India the gap between the rich and the poor still remains. So nobody can take it for granted that our future will be something easy, something without much problem—no. Problems are bound to happen. Then, here, in order to face the complicated world, we need two things, I believe.

Firstly, education. Our approach should be realistic to any problem. We should have a fuller knowledge about reality. Only then, we can get satisfactory results. No matter how noble our goal is, if the method used is unrealistic, you will not get to the goal satisfactorily. So, in order to carry a realistic approach, in order to know the reality fully, education has a very important role, because I believe the very purpose of education is to reduce the gap between appearance and reality.

And then, there is another factor. I usually stress that in order to see reality, we must look at it objectively. Even if it's something positive, desirable, what we want, if we look at that goal with attachment, you can't say that is reality. Here I want to share a story. Many years ago in Argentina, I had a meeting with some religious leaders and at least one scientist—one physicist—who I was told was a Chilean. At that meeting he mentioned he was a scientist, but that he believed he should not develop attachment toward his own scientific field. That's I think very important. Now, for example, I'm a Buddhist. I have faith toward Buddhism.

But I should not be attached toward the Buddhadharma. If I develop an attachment toward Buddhism, then my mind becomes biased. Through that way, I can't see the value of other religious traditions. So you must be very objective, unbiased.

So, therefore, in order to keep our minds neutral when we carry out research work, there should be no emotions like attachment, hatred, anger—these emotions are a hindrance to developing a calm mind. So we have to pay more attention to the emotional world. Usually we do not pay much attention, and that creates a problem. Various different religious traditions try to minimize these destructive emotions such as anger and hatred. All religions carry the teachings of love, compassion, forgiveness, and tolerance.

So we should, through using common sense, try to reduce these distinctive emotions. That's also very possible. I want to share one study with you. According to ancient Indian tradition, intelligence is the first level of knowledge. Knowledge through learning, through books, through lectures and other's words is one level of knowledge. Now, that's not very stable. You learn something and you develop certain concepts purely on the basis of imitating others. Then, if another person says, "No, that's wrong," your view also immediately changes. So, the first level of knowledge is very unstable. However, it acts as a basis. Then, we need further contemplation.

Analyze by yourself what you learned from others, or from books. When a certain point is mentioned by another person or a book, make sure you analyze and examine it. Then you develop second level of knowledge through your own analysis. That knowledge now much stronger. Now if another person says, "This is wrong," you will respond, "No. I have thoroughly investigated, I thoroughly studied this—it is true." So that is a kind of conviction. Then, the third level of knowledge is not to remain on an intellectual level of understanding, but to familiarize yourself with what you learn, so you eventually gain some experience. Knowledge through experience—now that's really solid. Then comes the calm mind. Here, I feel there are two methods to it. One method is, whenever we look at a certain thing, we must look in a more holistic way. That means you can't see the whole picture on one dimension. You must look from different angles or all the six dimensions; only then you get the clearer picture about reality. And then also, the ups and downs of our mental level usually take place when we see some positive or negative things. If the negative things are almost absolute, then there will be too much up and down. And if the positive things are always almost absolute, again there is much disturbance. In reality, it is impossible that one single thing is either full of positive or full of negative. Any event is relative. So compare certain other factors—compare this positive and compare that negative. Compare everything like that. For a holistic view, you must be able to see the different aspects of reality—that is how our minds can become more balanced.

The second necessary thing for a calm mind is warm-heartedness and compassion. As I mentioned earlier, all major religious traditions carry the same message, but essentially affection is a biological factor and does not come through religious faith. Look at animals—mammals or even birds—their young ones' survival depends entirely on the mother's care. This affection comes forth as a biological factor. There is a tremendous affection from the mother's side, which gives her the energy to take care, even the willingness to sacrifice her own life for the sake of her youngsters. Unless that kind of a strong emotion exists, the energy will not come. That emotion comes from biological resources—it is necessary.

From the child's perspective, as soon as it is born—without reason, without knowledge—it is biologically entirely dependent on its mother. As long as the mother cuddles it and carries it around, the child feels happy and safe. As soon as they separate, it feels unhappy. So we can say with certainty that affection comes from a biological factor—take that as a seed. Then, with the help of human intelligence, that affection can enrich and strengthen the child. Now, here are the differences. The first level of affection or compassion is biased. You cannot extend your affection to your so-called enemy, whose attitude toward you is negative and harming you. On that level, since that biased biological affection is action-oriented, you cannot extend your feeling of love and compassion toward the action which is negative toward you.

Then, through training and with the help of your human intelligence, you can analyze the pros and cons of affection, hatred and jealousy. Once you do that, you can develop conviction and warm-heartedness. An altruistic attitude is of immense benefit to the self, the family, the community and even to your health. Through analysis and with the help of your human intelligence, you can extend that biased, limited compassion until it is uplifted to an unbiased compassion—no longer action-oriented but oriented toward being itself . . . or in case of human beings, oriented toward human beings themselves. Today your enemy, as far as action or attitude is concerned, is negative toward you—but he is still a human being. He is part of the larger community on which your future depends. As you understand these things, you must maintain genuine compassion. A genuine sense of concern for the well-being of even your enemy—regardless of what their attitude is—is unbiased genuine compassion.

All major religious traditions teach us this lesson, but even without touching on religion, by using common sense, experience, and the latest scientific findings, we can develop conviction. We can develop this kind of infinite altruistic attitude toward others. Some nonbelievers are willing to sacrifice their own lives for the sake of others. That does not come through religious faith but through common sense. I think we can promote that through education, not through religious teaching but through awareness. The education system which we are using in this country was essentially introduced by the British. In the West, when separate institutions were started, for the moral ethics side, the church took responsibility; and people were also guided by family values to some extent. But now, in modern times, the influence of the church has reduced. Family values have also grown slacker. Back then, the educational institutions were taking care of only brain development; others were taking care of moral ethics.

Today, since the others' influence has reduced, the educational institution alone has the responsibility of both taking care of brain development and the growth of warm-heartedness. So now, in Europe and also in America and Canada, people in different universities are now showing genuine concern about the fact that in the modern education system, they do not pay adequate attention to warm-heartedness. In some countries with a Judeo-Christian background, people believe that moral ethics must be based on religious faith; whereas in this country, there are the secular ethics—in fact, India's constitution itself is based on secularism. Because of the circumstances of this country, there are so many different religious traditions. So if moral ethics are based on religious faith, the next question is what religion or faith should they follow? More complications. Therefore, you see, in India there must be ethics without a particular religious faith. That is, I think, a really useful concept.

Otherwise, when I talk in different parts of the world about secular ethics, some my friends have a little reservation about the very word "secularism." So I usually explain, according to

India, secularism doesn't mean disrespect for religion but rather a respect for all religions, isn't it? I think this is an advantage for India—so now we should promote the education of ethics according to a secular basis. I want to share with you that I always am telling the outside world, "India has the ancient wisdom, and I'm not talking about mystical things. I'm simply talking about ahimsa—non-violence. It is a thousand-year-old tradition, and very much in the Indian blood." And with that, religious harmony has also been there for a thousand years in this country. So, now today, all major world religious traditions established in this country live harmoniously. There is occasionally some problem between the Hindus and the Muslims, but that's quite understandable. In a billion human beings, some mischievous people would always be there. That's understandable, but basically, the atmosphere is very peaceful. All major religious traditions live peacefully.

The other day, in Jodhpur, I met a Romanian man who I just came across in a hotel. He told me he carried out some research work about religious harmony in this country. He spent some time in a village where all the villagers were Muslim, except three Hindu families. He was surprised at the very smooth relations. There was no threat to these three Hindu families from the majority of the Muslim community. So I told him, India, as a whole—south India, north India, east, west—they are all at the grassroots level—Hindu families, Muslim families, Christian families, and some Jains, and in some cases you see a few Buddhists. This is really India's treasure. It is not newly invented, but kept through the last thousand years. So, ahimsa—non-violence—and religious harmony—these are the two things I consider ancient Indian treasures. Wherever I go, I always talk about these two things, and I consider myself a messenger of ancient Indian thought.

In the meantime, I also talk to my Indian boss—that means Indians whom I consider my guru, and we are their chelas. Sometimes I mention that we are not only Indian guru's chelas, but also quite reliable chelas. The reason? In the last thousand years, the Nalanda tradition has had too many ups and downs in its own home. During those periods, we—your chelas—kept this Nalanda tradition intact. So, that shows we are quite reliable as chelas. So in any way, at the level of chela and messenger, I am quite active in promoting these things. Now my guru—my boss—must come, and should be more active regarding the promotion of non-violence and religious harmony. Particularly in the universities, each student should have clear picture about these, a clear realization of your own thousand-year-old treasure. Then India will become the greatest democratic country—population-wise, and also because of its stability.

I think in the early period, Mahatma Gandhi and the other Indian freedom fighters eventually spread the word about ahimsa to the outside world. Martin Luther King followed Mahatma Gandhi's path, and fought for and achieved American civil rights. Today, even the president of that country is a black American. These are real big changes. Luther King's wife once told me that Martin Luther King was so attracted to Gandhiji's lifestyle that he even wanted to dress like Mahatma Gandhi. That is a little bit too far, I think. (*Laughs*) And as you can see, Nelson Mandela—the first president of South Africa after it got its democracy—was also attracted to Mahatma Gandhi's non-violent principles.

With non-violence and religious harmony, I think, Indians should show the rest of the world that different religious traditions can live peacefully, learn from each other, with mutual respect and exchange of wisdom. I think India can show this to the rest of the world. However, in India, sometimes differences and problems have also been caused in the name of religion, both in history and in modern times. So, you—as my boss, my guru—should take a more active role in these fields.

In the meantime, within the country, discrimination is also caused by the caste system and the dowry system. Different treatment of the male and the female and the caste discrimination are also part of your tradition, but these are outdated. You must change these things. So the people—the youth—of this country, now you should take more initiative. Change some of these drawbacks. You must be active—that's I think very, very important. Lastly, sometimes take a little constructive criticism from your chela. Sometimes you're a little bit lazy. So you should be more hard-working—you should be full of self-confidence and work harder. That is all I want to tell you. So, thank you. Now I will take some questions.

QUESTIONS

QUESTION: *What do you think is the real purpose of life, and is it that when a person follows the path of spirituality and social work he attains the greatest happiness?*

HIS HOLINESS: Purpose of life? I think that's a rather mysterious question. I think there are different answers according to different philosophical concepts. If you believe in a religion that has a concept of God or creator, then I think you should ask God what the purpose of our life is.

And according to the non-theistic religions like Buddhism, Jainism, and also one part of Sankhya, which have no concept of creator but of self-creation, there is the law of causality, very similar to Darwinian theory. These three non-theistic religions developed only in this country—no other place. *So I believe the purpose of our life is happiness.* Simple reason—there's no guarantee of a good future, but we live on hope; we hope for the good. If anyone completely loses hope, then that very attitude shortens your lifespan, and in the worst case, you may commit suicide. Therefore, we survive here on the basis of hope—something good. So I can say the purpose of our life is to live a happy life.

Spirituality—spiritual life—as I mentioned earlier, can be lived on two levels. One is the secular level, without religious faith. In the first line of moral ethics, without touching upon religion, spirituality means taking care of your own mental peace. That's one level of spirituality. So naturally, wealth, money or diamond rings will not bring you inner peace, only the illusion that you feel, "I'm rich, I'm happy." But if you kiss your ring, the ring has no ability to respond to your affection. Dogs or cats, if you show them kindness, affection—even they have the ability to respond your affection. So we are living beings, we need affection. Matter has no ability to show us affection. So a life based on material value, which has no ability to give you affection, is illusion.

We are living beings. We must receive constant affection, only then does life become much more meaningful, much happier deep inside. Therefore, talking about these inner values is spirituality. Not talking about next life, not talking about nirvana, moksha, heaven, God, creator, no. Simply, how to live happily with inner peace—that's the way of spiritual life. I like that.

QUESTION: *According to you, which are the most important values that can be inculcated in any individual, and how can we achieve that? We've already talked about education. Which are the other important values that we can inculcate in ourselves?*

HIS HOLINESS: Basically, we are social animals. Each member, their future and their survival depend on the community. We are like bees, or ants, which have no religion, no constitution, no government organization, no police force, but they work together, simply because of the biological impulse to survive. So we are also social animals. It does not matter if one simple human being is very powerful. But his or her life, basic survival, depends on the rest of the community. This is a fact.

And you must have a close link with the community as the basis of your own future. For a happy life, you need to have a concern for the well-being of others. That sense of concern which really brings together I usually call affectionate attitude. So, you see, you need a sense of community or belonging. That's the ultimate source of our affection. And that is one key factor for being a social animal, so I talk about it often.

Of course, religious faith is individual business. But the entire humanity needs that sense of well-being of the community. I think, in the ancient times, each nation or community was more or less independent. Now today, due to the global economy and environmental issues and many other factors, the entire nearly seven billion human beings have come to be just one human family, one community. Today, not only nations but even continents are heavily interdependent.

According to that reality, we must have the concept of "the whole world is part of me." The centuries-old concept is of "we and they." But that concept divided "us" from "them," and on that basis, there was exploitation, harm, even war. In today's reality, everybody is a part of you, part of me, part of a big "we." So the concept of war is outdated. As long you have a genuine sense of concern for the well-being of another, there is no concept of killing, no concept of stealing, no basis of abuse, sexual abuse or rape, or of telling a lie or deception. As long as you have a strong feeling of concern for the well-being of others, all this negative physical or verbal action will not affect you—there is no room for these negative actions. So I feel, whether a person believes in some deeper values or not, at the practical level, if he follows these practices out of awareness, he becomes a really sensible person, and through that way he can build a happier world. This is my fundamental belief.

QUESTION: *Your Holiness, you spoke of peace and social welfare. My question is, how does capitalism relate to social welfare, and what role can capitalism play especially in the aftermath of the global recession?*

HIS HOLINESS: That's a difficult question. You should research. Personally, in 1954–55, I spent several months in Peking, studying Marxism and socialism. I am very attracted to the Marxist economy. Its emphasis is on equal distribution, so that is correct moral ethics; whereas capitalism talks simply about making more profit. So at that time, I told the Chinese Communist authority that I wanted to join the Chinese Communist Party. Even now, as far as socio-economic theories are concerned, I'm a Marxist. No confession, no secret—I have always made this clear.

But then, in today's China, of course, genuine Marxist socialism is no longer there. Today, it looks as if the Chinese Communist Party is without communist ideology. It is capitalist-communist— something very new. I'm wondering, Indian communist parties. I was told that some leaders of the Indian communists or Marxists have a very bourgeois lifestyle in their personal lives.

So, it looks like the socialist idea takes care of interests of the majority of the people, including the working-class people, needy people; this is very right. However, before things were being changed, both China and the former Soviet Union, in the economic field, were stuck nations. So really dynamic forces like capitalism are also necessary. I think the best solution is some kind of regulation—I don't know. When the eastern European countries had newly become independent, immediately after the Soviet collapse, I visited the then-Czechoslovakia on the invitation of President Havel—almost the first foreign visitor to come to that country. I said at that time, as I express now, that maybe these eastern European countries should research more and come up with a new synthesized political system, taking something from socialism and something from capitalism. But nobody took the suggestion seriously; and these countries also follow the Western capitalist system now. So I don't know. That's my view, but I have no clear answer for your question. More research work is necessary in that regard.

QUESTION: *Your Holiness, it's a great honor to have you here. My question to you is, in a world that looks into technological gadgets and social networking, what roles do you think art, culture, and music play?*

HIS HOLINESS: Actually, all of my talks are part of a culture of peace and non-violence. I think that, also, the artistic way—painting or some music or some songs—can carry a certain message and is very powerful medium.

I don't think people are losing interest in culture. Just after the morning session, an Indian journalist asked me about cricket: "Who will win the World Cup?" So people are watching these sports. And then different kinds of music—I think millions of people are really showing interest in that. I myself have no interest. I have no interest in music; I have no interest in any kind of sports. Of course when I was very young, I played Ping Pong or badminton, but now no longer. (*Laughs*) Of course these are, I feel, an important part of our life. And in the meantime, I also have the feeling that if we rely too much on the satisfaction of music or play, we are wasting our inner abilities. We end up depending heavily on external factors for inner peace. If you do that, then you only feel happy as long as the music or the picture is there; when these things are no longer around, you feel empty and bored.

On the other hand, inner peace is achieved without depending on sensorial experiences but entirely using mental ability, so that whether there is some external facility or not, you will always be peaceful and enjoy yourself. That is what I feel. This is why the people who spend their solitude in a remote place can still feel very happy—with no music, no television, nothing but ~~through~~ their inner meditation or other exercises to get immense inner peace. Days, nights, and months go on like that way. Of course the external facility is very good, but too much reliance on these things is not good. This is what I feel.

QUESTION: *Good afternoon, Your Holiness. In today's world of globalization and technological advancement, should the youth of India follow and totally rely upon the Indian traditions as mentioned by you, like learning from the Mahabharata and the Ramayana, and should we combine the best of the Western philosophies and the Indian philosophies in order to grow and develop?*

HIS HOLINESS: I have the view that technology—now universal—originally comes from the West. Technology provides us with physical comfort. India also needs that, particularly in the rural areas. I have always had the strong feeling that the real transformation of India must take place in rural India; not in some buildings, some factories, and some modern facilities in Bombay, Hyderabad, Allahabad, or Bangalore. Of course these are national interests, it is important; but the real change must take place in rural areas. That's very, very important.

Recently I was in Jaipur, or near Jaipur—at the Barefoot College there. At that college, illiterate old village people—mainly mothers—train in making solar electricity and things like that. These things are really wonderful. Then also near Nagpur, many years ago, I visited Dr. Ramdev. Also, on a few occasions, I have visited rural areas in Kerala and Gujarat. I think the few people who are really working in the rural areas—in education and in some handicrafts works—are doing something really very necessary. Because of them, India also receives the benefit of greater development in the technological field. The farm system must mechanize, otherwise it is difficult to feed everyone. The population is increasing, but the land cannot extend.

In the meantime, as I mentioned before, the Indian civilization is at par with the Egyptian civilization and the Chinese civilization—academics originally compare these three civilizations. I think the Indian civilization has much more sophisticated philosophical views about the mind. So these are the treasures of not only India but a treasure of the world, and must be preserved. Material development, which gives us physical comfort, and spiritual development, which provides us with mental comfort—these two must combine. So you must combine Western technology and modern education, as well as preserve your own thousand-year-old traditional values. You have a special role and a special responsibility. Whatever way I can serve you—however I can help you as a chela of your guru—it is my duty. Whatever way.

QUESTION: *The world has recently seen a huge global recession at the hands of a few greedy businessmen. How can ancient wisdom help overcome this shortcoming in our present and future business leaders?*

HIS HOLINESS: Business people also come from society. If we build a society which talks only of material values, the people who come from that particular society will naturally talk only of materials. So, we need some change in the fundamental level. Now in the West, some educationists are really questioning the existing educational system. A few decades ago, the number of people I noticed among businessmen who showed a concern about spirituality or inner peace was very low. Now there are more and more people among the business class who do it. And occasionally they organize my talks about inner values.

I think some of the big Indian companies also now will follow this trend. That's also good. Everybody cannot be a big businessman. But in the meantime, we should not forget about the basic well-being of society, and particularly, I hope, pay more attention to the education system and the economic conditions in rural areas. I think the media also has the responsibility to inform people about not only money values but other values, so that these businessmen are occasionally reminded that they are also getting sick, getting older, and then finally, they have to go. No matter how big the billionaire is, his money remains in the bank. He cannot carry it with him—only his mind.

So, educate, remind people, educate the media people. Our education systems should start educating us about secular ethics, from kindergarten right up to the university level. Then, I think, in the later part of this twenty-first century, humanity's way of thinking may change.

2

HEALTHY BODY, HEALTHY MIND

Kangra, 2012

I always speak in an informal way as it complements my broken English. I don't like to be very formal. I think that we are same the human being physically, mentally, and emotionally. The importance of a person is a creation of the mind. When we treat others as brothers and sisters, then it makes us happy.

It is a great honor to come to this important conference. For the last fifty-two years, I have been living at Dharamshala, before which I stayed at Mussoorie; thus, this area feels like my home. Back in 1961, when I reached Mcleodganj, it had only two shops. But over the years, the place has developed a lot. Now, there are many shops, restaurants, hotels, education centers, and medical centers. Everybody is concerned about health, which makes having medical centers really important. It is everybody's duty to take care of their own health. I believe that your work—all those who are in medical field—is very important work. But being in the profession is not enough; one should work with warm-heartedness. It is the best practice in the world, as you cure people and give them new life.

In Tibet, the doctors have good knowledge but don't have compassion, which does not make them very good doctors. In the medical profession, it's very important to have a genuine sense of concern for your patients. When I went to a hospital, the doctor was warm toward me and I felt happy to realize that they would take care of me. If the doctor or nurses don't smile, the patient may feel scared. It is important for the doctor to gain the trust of the patient, as that speeds up the recovery time.

India is the most populated democratic country in the world, with a long cultural and philosophical history that is almost five thousand years old. It has thousand-year-old traditions like ahimsa and religious harmony. In different parts of the world, we see a lot of unrest, violence, and injustice. Many areas are facing war in name of religion. India's concepts of ahimsa and religious harmony are relevant in today's world and are the solution to the unrest in the world. It helps develop respect for others' lives.

For thousands of years, India has been the birthplace for many religions, philosophies, and practices like Buddhism, Jainism, and Sikhism. Different religions have come from outside India like Christianity, Islam, and Judaism. The Zoroastrians came and settled here, and today, the Parsi community in Bombay exists in small numbers but is very happy. Due to the existence and practice of so many religions in one country, religious harmony has become a very relevant issue. Indians should feel proud of their rich cultural heritage. Since 1947, India adopted the democratic system, which is very stable. During Emergency there was anxiety but after elections the government changed smoothly and peace was restored by Morarji Desai.

British imperialism introduced a very good education system. Many of you look young, and it is your duty to work hard and use the rich tradition as a strong weapon. There are many countries that are in competition with India, thus one needs to work hard and with courage and self-confidence to make sure that the country stays ahead of all. These days I consider myself a messenger of India's thoughts, like ahimsa. I have spent the last fifty-three years of my life in this country. A group of Chinese reporters once asked me that why I refer to myself as a son of India—they thought that was a political reason behind it. I told them that, as a child, I have read the teachings of Buddhism in Sanskrit as well as my local language. I also follow the teachings of the Nalanda University. Then my body has survived on Indian dal, rice, and chapatti for so long. Thus, I consider myself a son of India. The Chinese journalists understood.

I feel a serious concern about corruption. When I visited Rajasthan last year, a student asked me if it was true that in real life one had to take part in corruption, or otherwise they would never succeed. Such thought of corruption in a young mind is disturbing to me. When I was in Bombay, a businessman friend of mine mentioned that without corruption, one could not succeed in business. In other countries, which have no moral principles, corruption is understandable. But in this country with so many religious-minded people, it is a matter of concern.

I tease my Indian friends that they put flowers in front of their deities and recite shlokas without knowing their meaning. If you are a true follower, follow the teachings of that God. No religion preaches that you should lead a life with corruption, lie, kill, steal, and so forth. All major religions say that one must practice love, compassion, honesty, and forgiveness. I tell people to be clear about their beliefs. If they believe in religion, they should lead their life honestly. If they worship money, then they will have to lead a corrupted life and regret earning a bad name among their peers.

A few days ago, I met a religious Cuban refugee who said that he always prayed to God to send all dictators to heaven, which showed that he still had some respect for them, since he wanted them to go to heaven and not hell. I have always advised people to follow ahimsa, work hard, and live honestly, which will bring them respect from the community and also from their genuine friends. If you are a hypocrite, then the trust between friends will not be there, and you will be unhappy.

I think, for good health of the body, one needs to have a calm mind and a warm heart. With the help of a calm mind and confidence, a person can face any adversity in life. A healthy body and a healthy mind go hand in hand. Medicines alone may not help a lot. The basic strengths that everyone needs to have to succeed are values, hard work and a modern approach in every field. Indians can make a significant contribution through hard work, knowledge and confidence, which can help develop the country internally and internationally.

I am in my late seventies and may not stay to see the changes. All those younger than me, with healthy vision and hard work, may enjoy the good results. Even after my death, either from heaven or hell, I will check whether you are implementing these advices properly or not. My young companions here and I will watch together, and if you don't work, then we will punish you. Thank you!

QUESTIONS

QUESTION: *Is forgiveness more important than punishing? You mentioned in the session that if the youth do not perform their duties correctly, then you will punish them even after you have gone to heaven. In the light of this statement, is forgiveness more important that punishment?*

HIS HOLINESS: Forgiveness means that despite some wrongdoing, you will not keep an ill-feeling. Instead, you should feel a genuine sense of concern for those who are doing wrong. That, I think, is forgiveness. In the meantime, also from a genuine sense of concern for their future, some punishment might have good result. For example, when the Chinese torture our Tibetans, we develop a concern for their future. According to the concept of karma in spirituality, those who have accumulated negative karma will face bitter consequences in their life. Even though we do oppose their control, mentally we are compassionate toward them. That is the practice of forgiveness.

QUESTION: *I am a doctor. I do everything that makes me a good human being like have compassion and not neglect my duties. I am at peace with myself. Will it help me further if I take recourse to spirituality in rendering my duties? Will it further my mental enhancement?*

HIS HOLINESS: Yes, in a medical profession you should do your duty with knowledge and genuine concern for the well-being of your patient. Action depends on motivation on the mental, the physical, and the verbal levels—if the motivation is positive, all the levels become positive. I think my first commitment is to promote human value and secular ethics. Secularism means paying respect to all traditions and also to nonbelievers. Once, L. K. Advani told me that a thousand-year-old tradition prescribed by Charvaka denies God or dharma, but believes in the existence of reality. The rest of the spiritual thinkers criticized that view, but still referred to him as a rishi. It is a clear sign of respect. I believe that seven billion people cannot all be equally serious about spirituality. For personal interest, personal moral ethics or inner value, one must inculcate them—it is for their own benefit. Love, compassion, and forgiveness are meant to be practiced by both believers and nonbelievers. A person needs to remain honest, as honesty is a part of spirituality.

QUESTION: *The body is independent, and so is the mind. When the body perishes, does the mind also perish along with the body? If not, where does it go?*

HIS HOLINESS: For the past thousands of years, much research has been conducted on the subject, and many answers have come up. Now, for those who believe that God is the creator, they believe that the spirit remains after the death for the final judgment (whether the person will go to hell or heaven). The Indian religion—including Sankhya—is an ancient system of thought which believes that Lord Brahma is the creator. They also believe in rebirth and karma. Buddhism and Jainism followers don't believe in any creator, beginning or end.

Most religions except Buddhism believe in "atma," which is like a ghost that survives even after physical function and the mind cease to exist. Buddhism believes in a combination of the body and the mind, and many different levels of each. After death, as soon as the heart stops, within a short period of time the brain stops working, too; but a certain level of the body and another of the mind don't cease to work. The deepest level of he mind survives even after death. I know a few cases where the body remained very fresh for weeks after death. Modern scientists don't have any answer for this. After thirty years of dialogue with scientists, some of them are showing interest in the subject and are conducting experiments. The Buddhist explanation of the deepest level of the mind and the Hindu explanation of the atma are very similar.

QUESTION: *You mentioned honesty. Everyone claims to be honest, but has their own definition. What is the definition of honesty according to you these days?*

HIS HOLINESS: The human mind is very sophisticated. Thus it can take out different interpretations of the definition of moral ethics. One tends to be more honest when they deal with cats or dogs, because if they are shown genuine sincerity, then the feelings are reciprocated. Wealthy or poor, educated or not educated, everybody needs to be truthful.

The Indian theory about the mind, according to the Pali or the Nalanda tradition, is very rich. If a person is truthful and transparent in his intentions and respects others, then there will be no room in the mind for thoughts like cheating or lying. The source of honesty is love and compassion. One level of love is biological, like the mother's love, which is biased. But love and compassion should be shared among all, even to one's enemies. Any action that brings trust is honest.

QUESTION: *It is human behavior that we are not content with what we have achieved in life. This leads to encroaching on others' rights and creating disharmony in the society. What, according to you, should we do to remain content and bring peace and harmony in society?*

HIS HOLINESS: My answer to that question is secular ethics. Material value has limitation, as a person only desires to own more of it, but only encounters dissatisfaction. There is a story about a king who wanted more. But things related to the mind, like knowledge, have no limitations. After the global economy crash, a friend who is an economist told me that no one wanted any crisis, but crisis was ultimately their own creation. The reason, he said, was greed—the kind of greed that makes one go blind. It's all speculation that creates such situations, with no sense of reality. So contentment comes from a realistic approach. If one thinks that he has enough things, then his mental attitude will give him a calm mind.

I tease my businessmen friends that they are slaves of money. In Moscow, Russia, a businessman told me that he wanted to go to Los Angeles, USA, and return to Moscow that very day—and I thought, so much traveling, only for profit? Profit does not benefit a person mentally or physically. But at a national level, the priorities change. There are many poor people in India. Even though diseases like polio are eradicated (as I saw on BBC), medical facilities are still poor. India still needs development. I went for a meeting where I realized that very few people think of the future. They should get inspired by the great Indian leaders like Nehru and Gandhi who started the trend of ahimsa for everyone's good.

QUESTION: *In Bhutan they have an indicator—gross national happiness—which is an indicator of the health and economy of the population. Would you like to suggest it to the policy makers who are sitting next to you to adopt it as an indicator for India?*

HIS HOLINESS: It's very easy to suggest this, but for real development a lot of work is required, mainly in the field of education. This year, Delhi University is doing research so that they can make secular ethics a part of the education system. Modern education lacks something which shapes our mind, so it needs to undergo some changes. Along with education, economy is an important issue too. The gap between poor and rich is so great that it is morally wrong.

At Dharamsala, near a construction site, I spoke to a laborer from Chandigarh—a lady with children. She told me that nobody wanted to leave their village but they needed the work. Real transformation should take place in rural areas to reduce the gap between the rich and the poor.

Part Four

INNER AND
OUTER PEACE

1

Peace through Inner Peace

Minneapolis, 2011

Respected president of this famous, great university of (*asks translator*) Minnesota—(*audience laughs*) I have to confirm these names, these things—my mind is not very reliable or good at details. You are giving me this honorary degree, so thank you very much. I often say, when I receive this kind of an honorary degree, that I already have a special high degree, achieved without study. I'm sure ordinary people, in order to get that kind of a degree, need a lot of effort. And then, special thanks for this hat. Sometimes I notice that the people who have bald heads prefer hats. I do not want to hide my baldness. (*Laughs*) So, after ten years, once more, I'm here. And each time people really show genuine, human, warm feeling. I very much appreciate that.

From my side also, whenever I meet people, no matter what their culture, no matter what their faith, nationality, or color, I always emphasize the importance of the fundamental level on which we are the same human being—mentally, emotionally, physically we are the same. And, more importantly, everyone—including animals and insects—wants a peaceful life, does not want disturbances, and everyone has the right to have a happy, successful life. And then, of course, an educational institution such as this is very, very important, because our human brain has great potential for increased knowledge.

So institutions such as this university, I think, offer tremendous help to grow this potential. Modern education system, as far as I know, started about a thousand years ago in the European continent, as separate educational institutions. At that time, religious institutions took care of the moral, spiritual, and ethical sides of the mind. Religious institutions took the full responsibility for this spiritual side. And, also, I think there was much emphasis on family values. So, at that time, the newly developed, newly established educational institutions cared only about brain development and education. Time passed and the influence of the Church also declined a little, as did family values. Therefore, the educational institution itself now should take care of both these aspects—of knowledge and warm-heartedness. So here, it seems that we do not adequately pay attention to developing and maintaining the compassionate human mind.

We are at the beginning of the twenty-first century. Generally speaking, I think both the modern material condition and modern education are very highly developed. However, that does not necessarily reduce the human problem. For example, in human history, I think the twentieth century was the most important. During that century, a lot of inventions and innovations took place in the fields of science and technology mainly; also in the economy and in education, much has developed.

However, according to some historians, within the twentieth century, the number of people who were killed through violence, through war—even through civil war—was around two hundred million. I think of all these past centuries, the biggest number of casualties through violence was in the twentieth century. And also, I think, as a result of inventions in technology and science, nuclear weapons were developed and unfortunately, during the Second World War, two such bombs were used on human beings.

I have had the opportunity to visit both Hiroshima and Nagasaki. In my previous visit, when I reached the center of the explosion, I saw they had created a small museum at that terrible scene. At the museum, there was a burnt watch that had stopped at 10 a.m. and a bunch of needles that were melted. Also, I met some old patients who had become sick because of the radiation from the nuclear bomb. This immensely destructive weapon brought more fear and anxiety to this planet—the really marvellous achievements of the human brain brings more fear to the world. So, what's wrong—knowledge? Oh, knowledge is marvellous. But then, I fear the moral principles are lacking. So therefore, because of our past experience, I think that now the time has come for us to think about how to cultivate and sustain a sensible set of moral ethics.

What are moral ethics? I feel the very word "moral" is related with the mind and emotions, and not with matter. We can't say, on the basis of matter, that moral is difficult. Moral is related to mental quality. So, certainly, those minds or emotions or motivations that bring comfort, happiness, and joyfulness, that is a moral thing. Motivation, or emotion, which brings fear, pain, distrust, these are immoral. So, we human beings, are social animals, and for survival, need human communities. That is human nature. Nature created us as social animals, so genuine cooperation is very essential. Even small insects or birds or animals have no religion, no constitution, no government, but by nature, they work together, and cooperate.

We are also, basically, social animals and really need cooperation. But genuine cooperation cannot develop by force, by money, by power—it is entirely based on friendship. Friendship is entirely based on trust and trust is based on open-heartedness. If you look at the other openly and honestly, speak, and act honestly and truthfully, that brings trust. Trust brings friendship; and friendship brings genuine harmony and cooperation. So, I think, the basic element for openness or trust is warm-heartedness.

If you consider that others, just like you, want happiness and do not want suffering, you will see that it is illogical to harm, cheat, and lie to others. If you receive a lie from someone, you feel uncomfortable. So, according to our own experience, we must avoid any physical, verbal, mental action which brings fear, harm, or makes others uncomfortable. These are immoral. Physical, mental, and verbal actions which bring happiness and joyfulness—not only temporarily but also for long term—these things are moral.

So now the point is, by nature, we all have the potential for warm-heartedness, because we all come from our mothers, and we have grown up under our mothers' tremendous affection. We all have the same experience. That's very, very important. Tremendous affection at a very young age really makes a difference to your whole life. Now my own experience—I come from very remote area, the northeastern part of Tibet. My village, particularly, was very remote and my home was a farm. Both my parents were illiterate; however, my mother was very, very kind-hearted and a very good mother. Therefore, we, her children, grew up within that atmosphere. That I think really has an immense impact.

Sometimes, I jokingly tell my friends, my mother was more kind to me. I was the youngest of her children. Usually the mother extends love to all, but particularly to her youngest one. So that spoiled me a little, I think. In a village, the mother usually carries her child on her shoulder—my mother, too, used to carry me. She was so kind toward me that I became a little aggressive. So while I sat on my mother's shoulders, I held her two ears—when I wanted to go in this direction, I did this, and for that direction, I did that. (*Mimes pulling ears*) If my mother did not follow that way, then I cried and my legs did that. (*Mimes kicking*) So, in any way, I really feel a certain amount of my warm-heartedness originally comes from my mother.

And then, obviously, if we examine each individual thoroughly, those who outwardly appear knowledgeable are smart. But, at a deeper level, those who have received maximum affection from their mothers at a young age are more calm and less fearful—they have a sense of security. Someone may be very wise, educated or famous, but if they have received less affection or have been abused, deep inside them there is some sense of insecurity. Such people find it difficult to show others real affection. So their whole lives, deep inside, they carry some sense of loneliness—they are helpless. That's our common experience.

So we all have the potential for warm-heartedness, which we received from our mothers and our friends. Then, obviously, we watch people or our families. Families that are full of affection and friendship are quite happy even if they may not be very rich. Then, there are families that are very rich and powerful, but there is a suspicion, competition, and lack of real affection or trust among the family members. At the real human level of genuine happiness or satisfaction, they have much less. It's quite obvious.

And sometimes, I describe it as our inner door that opens, and through that way, you can easily communicate with other people and create friendships. On the other hand, an extremely self-centered attitude makes you close your inner door. It is difficult to communicate with other people. Also, when you think only of yourself, your entire mental outlook becomes very narrow. And with that narrow vision, even small problems appear unbearable to you. When you think more about the well-being of others and your mind gets a wider perspective, even quite a serious problem appears okay. It may still be unfortunate and bad, but it is okay, because your attitude widens. Too much self-centered thinking brings you more to the danger of heart attacks and depression.

To some extent, I also can tell you this from my own experience. I think my mental state comparatively is quite peaceful. Even when passing through some difficult periods, my mind stays quite calm. Not because it is dark—I think I have a quite sharp mind—but deep inside, there is the sense of affection and concern for the well-being of others. Also, I truly consider others as my brothers and sisters. They may have different views and interests, but they are still human beings. That kind of attitude is really of immense help to keep peace of mind, which is very helpful to keep a healthy body. So sometimes we call it healthy-mind-healthy-body. One must not only take care of a healthy body. Money, material facilities, and also, education mainly address the concern for material wealth, which is not adequate. There must be some project to study our minds and how to tackle these destructive emotions.

Now here, I usually feel that there are three ways to promote these inner values. One is theistic religion—the concept of God, which is very powerful to increase love and compassion. On one occasion in Jerusalem, I had a discussion with some teachers. One Jewish teacher told our conference that he often told his students, "When you meet people who usually irritate you, think that person is made in the image of God. It will help." So, among his students, there are some Palestinians and some Jews. Later some of the Palestinian students told him, "After we heard your advice and teaching, we practice it when we come close to Israeli checkpoints." One of my Muslim friends told me, as a genuine practitioner of Islam, you must extend your love to all creation. Since you respect and love Allah, you must extend your love toward his entire creation. This is a very logical, theistic approach.

Then, there are non-theistic religious traditions like Buddhism and Jainism. They follow the law of causality, so there is no God—no concept of a God or creator. According to that, if you help or do good things for another person, you get benefits. If you harm another person, you get negative consequences. That approach is also very helpful to increase a sense of concern of others' well-being.

Then there must be a third way, since these values we are talking about do not concern heaven, hell, or the next life. We are simply talking about well-being within this life—at the family and the community levels. As I mentioned earlier, first we learn from our mothers—whether we are believers or nonbelievers. So the instinct to give and receive love and this moral principle itself are secular, and not based on religious faith. Of course, all major religious traditions emphasize the importance of these things and there's a method to strengthening this practice and these values. But these values themselves are just human nature—a part of the human mind and human emotion. So since the object itself is, strictly speaking, secular, there is nothing to do with religion. Even animals appreciate affection. Animals also have the ability to look after their own youngsters. These are biological factors, not something acquired from religious teaching. So, it is something secular. Therefore, there should also be a way to promote this in a secular way.

As I mentioned earlier, depending on the fact we all come from our mothers, and using common sense, we notice that affectionate families are much happier. Scientific findings also support this observation. So, use these facts and develop awareness about the importance of these things, and you can develop conviction. Warm-heartedness is important for your own well-being, so that's a secular way to educate. Therefore, when I use the words "secularism" or "secular," it doesn't mean disrespect of religion but rather respect for all religions, including nonbelievers.

This is not new, you know, in India. Out of the three most ancient world civilizations—Egyptian, Chinese, and the Indus Valley—it seems the Indus civilization developed much more complex ideas about philosophical views. So for a thousand years in India, a different philosophical view called nihilism has existed. It believes in no God, no next life, no salvation—nothing except day-to-day life. That's what they call the nihilistic school of thought. The rest of the Indian schools of thought criticized the nihilistic view; but the person who believed in that school of thought was referred to as a "rishi," and rishi means "sage."

That's India's thousand-year-old tradition. You may have different views, and you can criticize and debate, but as a person, you must respect others. So one of my Indian friends—the former deputy prime minister of India—told me that one of the reasons India is very successful democracy is because of that tradition. India's understanding about secularism respects even the nonbeliever. That, I think, is very relevant to today's world. So when I use the word "secularism," please don't think that it is a negative attitude toward religion; but rather, it shows respect.

India is a thousand-year-old, multi-religious community, including several kingdoms, besides different home-grown religious traditions. All major religious traditions eventually found their home and settled there; even Zoroastrianism—whose followers are called Parsis—which originally came from Persia. Today in India, in one big city, Bombay, their whole population is less than 100,000; even smaller than the Tibetan refugee population. But they have kept their own religion. They always keep worshipping fire with no danger or threat.

Recently I met one European from Romania. She carried out some research about harmony in different religious traditions in India. And she told me that she was really surprised to find that in one village, where the Muslim community was large and there were only three Hindu families, the Hindu families faced no fear or threat. Everyone lived very happily and in close friendship. She was surprised. That's the Indian tradition—thousands of years of harmony among different religious traditions. And India's constitution itself, because of that reality, is based on secularism.

So, the problem is that some people believe moral principles must be based on religious faith, and complications arise because of that. In India, because of its reality of being a multi-religious society, if moral ethics were to be based on religious faith—which one would we choose? There would be a lot of complications. Some say there is God; some say there is no God. Simply based on secular moral ethics, it is much easier and better. That can be universal. Religious faith cannot be universal.

Here, I want to share one thing. According to religious traditions, the concept of one-truth-one-religion is very important. At the individual level, that's very relevant in order to boost your own faith. But in terms of the community, now, that one-truth-one-religion concept is not realistic. In terms of the community, different people have different faiths, including nonbelievers. Then how can you say that one's own religion is the only truth and the only religion? How to force that on others? That they should accept your religion is impossible. So therefore, realistically speaking, in the terms of the community, the concept of several-truths-several-religions is relevant.

Whenever I have an opportunity to talk about these things, I appreciate it very much. Now, this university has taken one more step forward in talking about spirituality and healing. I think that is very good. So I'm really looking forward to more progress and activities in that field. Within the next few years, I will return in order to check how much development has taken place.

In any case, I really appreciate the effort. A few other universities—like Wisconsin, Stanford, and Emory, as far as I know—are already carrying out some programs about the training of the mind and how much effect it has on the body, on the mind. Now, I've found a fourth university—the University of Minnesota. So now in the future, I will mention *four* universities are really carrying out serious research work in that respect. So I appreciate this opportunity very much. Thank you. That's all, thank you.

QUESTIONS

QUESTION: *By coincidence, the artist Ai Weiwei was planning on being here today but could not make it. What advice would you have for him and those who are working to make China a better place?*

HIS HOLINESS: Unfortunately, in recent years and particularly recent months, the Chinese government, due to its hard-line thinking, has placed a tighter control on intellectuals and artists. I think these people should look to the past, during and even before the Cultural Revolution. On a number of occasions, there was a lot of restriction and suppression of intellect. But intellect, I think, is a treasure of the human brain, so it cannot be controlled. For years, some of these people were put in prison or under house arrest, but then there were new intellectuals again, and even these would get freedom. So in China, the most populated nation in the world, with a long history and cultured, hardworking people, this tragedy sometimes comes and disappears. What is important is that the people—particularly those intellectual people—have no reason to feel hopeless or demoralized; they must keep their spirit and their enthusiasm.

QUESTION: *What is a healthy balance between attachment to one's home and non-attachment as taught by Buddhism? Please address this question on both a personal level—attachment to children—and on a societal level—attachment to the USA.*

HIS HOLINESS: There are two levels of concern for others. One level, as I mentioned earlier, is the biological factor. What you call compassion, or affection-oriented attitude, so therefore, that level of compassion can be developed only toward your friend, not your enemy, because an enemy's attitude is negative toward you. Now, with religious traditions, including Buddhism, when we talk about compassion, it is not oriented to their attitude, but the being, the creator itself. For example, some nurturing of yourself is not due to you being nice to yourself but because, spontaneously, you want happiness, you do not want suffering.

So others also, including your enemy, have the same desire and right to overcome suffering, to achieve happiness. On that basis, we can extend our compassion, so that compassion is unbiased. The previous kind of compassion is biased and very much related with attachment. The later part of the compassion is without attachment.

So one time, this quantum physicist mentioned to me that he should not develop attachment toward his own scientific field. That's really marvellous. In my own case, I'm Buddhist, but I should not develop an attachment toward Buddhism. If I develop an attachment toward Buddhism, then my mind becomes biased. Through a biased mind, I cannot see the another's value objectively. Buddhism never encourages the development of attachment. Attachment and compassion are two separate things.

So in order to develop unbiased, infinite love and compassion, first you must detach yourself. You must give equality to all—both enemies and friends. Then develop unbiased compassion. And then also it is often that people confuse Buddhism and some other religion, and consider desire as something negative. Desire with attachment is negative. We have to develop desire with reason, for example, the desire for the well-being of another, or the desire to overcome one's own suffering. That's right. Desire without proper basis is very much related to attachment. That kind of desire must reduce. And then, there is anger. There are different varieties of anger—anger with ill feeling is different from anger out of compassion or a sense of concern. Anger can also come from an egoistic attitude, which can lead to bullying and exploitation of others. That kind of egoistic attitude is negative. But another egoistic feeling—the sense of a strong self—is necessary. You need the sense of a strong self to develop courage and willpower. So in a mental or emotional world, there are so many varieties.

Nurturing yourself is not due to your being nice to yourself; it is because, spontaneously, you want happiness, you do not want suffering, so this sense of taking care comes. This is more positive. Even faith is a good thing, but faith in the wrong thing—blind faith—is dangerous. So faith exercised with wisdom and intelligence is very good. Faith exercised with just attachment is negative. So there are many varieties.

QUESTION: *This question is from a nine-year-old child—If you could completely solve one problem in the world, what would that be?*

HIS HOLINESS: I don't know. I think, in reality, there are so many varieties of the same problem that just one person cannot solve any of them. Everyone—over six billion human beings—has the responsibility to tackle these problems.

QUESTION: *What role do you see the Internet playing in helping people to experience and discover one heart, one mind, and one universe? What can we do to further this role?*

HIS HOLINESS: I think the Internet is one of the very advanced ways of communication. And I think, basically, in order to develop the human mind in the more complete form, we need a lot of information. Just one warning—one-sided information is very harmful, so we need a variety of information. If one concept calls something good and another calls it bad, we need both concepts. That gives us the opportunity to investigate by ourselves. So now today, in the information era, the Internet is wonderful. I think, because of that, a lot of positive change is taking place on this planet. Unlike say the early or mid-twentieth century, when there was much less information and therefore it was easier to develop unnecessarily negative emotion.

So information, which builds a clearer picture about the whole world, is of immense help. I always say when I meet the press that media people should have long noses—like the elephant's nose—and should smell both what's in front of them and, most importantly, what is behind, what is going on. That's very, very important. They must do a thorough investigation of what is happening and then inform the public, provided that they do it honestly, truthfully, unbiased, and objectively. That's very important, particularly in a democratic society. I am expressing that the world belongs to over six billion human beings—not to governments, and not to any one particular religion. For example, the USA belongs to people of the USA, not to the Democratic Party or the Republican Party.

Of course, it is impossible for all three hundred million people of a country to govern the country at the same time, so the better way is to choose some people through elections. A democratically elected government is really by the people and for the people. The best way to govern your own country is through a democratic system. And in order to make a democratic system work efficiently, according to moral principles, sometimes a constitution is very good. Everybody is equal under the law; yes, this country really practices that. However, sometimes the human brain is so clever that even in a very good system, different mishaps are known to happen. Therefore, media people are important. They need to make clear what is wrong, what is a corrupted mind, what corruption is going on and where. That's something the media people—not the government but public organizations like the media—must investigate and make clear.

In these fields, the Internet I think has a very important role. And as I'm always telling, media people also have a very important role to create more awareness of certain points which we usually neglect. Moral ethics is also one of them. I think the new technology and the spread of information is really wonderful. Of course, if you use it the wrong way, it also sometimes makes more trouble; but I think as far as you use it honestly, truthfully, and transparently, the more information, the better. If you have something to hide, this makes it difficult. If you are hypocritical in your ways, then you have to be very, very cautious.

QUESTION: *Do you think the world is getting better or worse, and why?*

HIS HOLINESS: Better. The reason is not only my observation. In 1996—around the end of the twentieth century—I had the opportunity of an audience with the late Queen Mother of England. Her own age was then ninety-six. She had been born at the beginning of the twentieth century, so in a way she observed almost a whole century. At that time, I had asked her, "Since you have observed almost the whole century, do you think the world is becoming better or worse, or is just the same?" Without hesitation, she told me that it was becoming better. When she was young, there were no concepts of human rights or the rights of self-determination. Now they are—now they have become universal. She gave these two as the examples of the indications that the world is getting better.

From my own experience, I think that in the early twentieth century, nobody talked about the importance of ecology. Now many people show genuine concern for the environment. That's wonderful. There are even political parties that are green parties. One time when I met people from this green party in New Zealand or some other country, I jokingly told them that if I remained in that country, I would have joined their green party.

In any case, these are, I think, signs of greater maturity. I think scientists are also now looking more seriously into the mind. Previously, scientists only studied hard science—only things which we can measure or calculate. The mind and feelings are something different. Now that modern science is slowly advancing, scientists are showing an interest in the consciousness—what the relation is between the brain and the mind. And also, I think there is more harmony among the religions. For example, Pope John Paul II convened the Assisi Meeting, where he invited the leaders of different Christian denominations and also some Buddhist and Hindu religious leaders. The idea of one-truth-one-religion is gradually changing into several-truth-several-religions. So these are, I think, clear signs of greater progress and civilization.

I also think the experience of education has really made a tremendous contribution to widening and opening up our minds, teaching us to see more holistically. What do you think? And then the word "compassion." Previously, in a politician's statements, I think compassion had no place. In the later part of the twentieth century, I remember one of the statements by Mrs. Thatcher where she mentioned compassion and then non-violence.

And in the early twentieth century, scientists, officials and governments were full of enthusiasm to build nuclear weapons. Now, people are talking of how to reduce and reach a total ban of nuclear weapons. These are signs of progress.

2

HOPE FOR A PEACEFUL WORLD

Yokohama, 2010

I am very happy to meet the Japanese youth because I always feel that people of my own generation belong to the twentieth century. The twentieth century is gone. With the twentieth century, we witnessed a century of bloodshed and violence. According to some historians, in the last century, over two hundred million people were killed through violence. Only in the later part of this century did a desire for peace and non-violence start. There is a feeling of resentment or fatigue about violence.

In that regard, you Japanese people have your own unique experience—during the Second World War you suffered immensely. Two nuclear bombs were experienced by the Japanese people at Hiroshima and Nagasaki. So you are people who must lead the world toward peace and against war, particularly against nuclear weapons. You—the young people aged twenty, thirty, and below—are the people of the twenty-first century. The twenty-first century is ten years past, but there are ninety years yet to come. What kind of century it will be is very much dependent on you. So I'm indeed happy meeting you, and for this exchange of views.

Now, I want to tell you, in different parts of the world, a number of people feel that humanity is basically negative in nature. Their view is that violence is part of human nature, and therefore our world is doomed. I think that's totally mistaken and wrong. In India, there are still pockets of violence, but if you look at the whole picture, one billion human beings seem to be living peacefully. The twentieth century had a lot of suffering, but we human beings are becoming more mature. There has been a big change in people's concepts of war from the early part of the twentieth century to the later part; also in the issue of the environment. In the early part of the century, generally there was no concern or awareness about the environment. At that time, people just liked to consume everything, without any awareness of the limitations of major resources. Even the concept of spirituality in the early part of the twentieth century included people only talking about material development. In the later part of the twentieth century, people began to feel that there's a limitation to material value—ultimately, peace of mind is very essential. So people are paying attention to the important of peace of mind. Whether believers or nonbelievers, more and more people are talking and thinking about the value of spirituality.

Also, in the early part of the twentieth century, a number of monarchies were dissolved. These are big changes within the scope of one century. Therefore, judging from the whole picture, humanity is becoming more mature and realistic, so therefore things are getting better and better.

These days, human rights and the right of self-determination are universal. I myself was born in 1935, so just at the beginning of the Second World War. The Japanese had already invaded China; wasn't it around 1935? I can't remember the exact date.

Anyway, the Second World War was about to start, and in Europe Nazi Germany had developed, followed by Mussolini in Italy—what you call the Fascist Party. After the Second World War came the Korean War, the Vietnam War, and so on—so it seems that in the early part of my life, the news was often full of war. And this immense violence failed to solve the human problem;

in fact, it only added to the problem. War, I think, uses violence in the maximum way, and instead of solving problems, it only plants the seeds of further problems. Now, unfortunately, the early part of the twenty-first century has been exactly the same. President Bush's sort of moderation is good—the aim, which is to bring democracy in Iraq, is good—but the method is violent, so unexpected consequences happen. These days, I feel humanity is becoming more mature and more realistic. Because of our own experience, now we pay more attention to certain fields that were previously neglected. Nobody knows what will happen to humanity after several thousand years, but I think, at least after the next century, and the one after that, and the one after it, humanity and our planet will certainly become more peaceful, compassionate, and happier.

There are possibilities there. But then it entirely depends on our own efforts and clarity of vision. Then, also, I can say that during the Second World War and the early part of the twentieth century, the nations were competing in the construction of nuclear bombs. In the later part of the century, the important nations—mainly the USA and the Russian federation—are now actually, seriously talking about reducing nuclear warheads and eventually a total ban on nuclear weapons. These are very, very positive signs. Because of that kind of a background, there is the real possibility of a better world. I am just another human being out of six billion. I always believe that everyone has the responsibility to think about the world. I am Tibetan, but we belong to six billion human beings, so we have to think about all the six billion—the whole planet.

You're Japanese. But now the time to talk about only Japan has gone. No. Now you must think and talk about the whole world, because Japan's future depends upon the rest of the world. In the ancient times—the eighteenth or nineteenth century, you see—nations were more or less independent of each other. They were something like self-sufficient. Today, that kind of situation has completely changed. Even Iraq is a powerful nation—their future depends on rest of the world. And look at the spirit of the European Union.

In the past century these small nations fought for their own sovereignty. The people of each nation were willing to sacrifice their own lives to save their sovereignty. Now they realize that common interest is more important than individual interest. The individual's interest is very much mixed with the common interest. Therefore after the Second World War, as a new concept, the

European Union created the euro. The German deutschemark is a very powerful currency, but they're willing to sacrifice it for the common currency. The Italian lira, like the Japanese yen, is not of much value. These things are a clear sign that people are getting more worried, and that they now realize that a wider interest is more important than self-centered interest. This is very important.

Now the Copenhagen Summit about global warming failed to bring concrete results. Why? Some important nations consider their national interests more important than global interests. That's why it failed. Some young nations are still thinking their national interests are more important than global interests. But in the world at large, things are changing. Therefore, I—as a one human being among six billion, with a sense of global responsibility—have two commitments. My number one commitment is promoting inner value.

Inner value means that from birth, biologically, we're equipped to showing affections to others. We have a sense of concern about others' well-being. From childhood, because of this biological factor, we already acquired these things. That is very, very precious, because we are social animals. Individual life depends on other members of the community, therefore emotionally, there is something which brings us together, endows us with human affection and compassion. So whether we believe or don't believe in God, these things are biologically equipped. According to the latest scientific findings, warm-heartedness is very important for a healthy body. Sometimes they say healthy-mind-healthy-body. This is true. Constant anger and fear are actually eating into our immune systems, according to some scientists. A calmer and more compassionate mind automatically brings inner peace. A calm mind is very essential for a healthy body. Therefore, these things I describe as human values. Wherever I go, I always try to make this clear. Money's important, but this inner sort of wealth is more important than external wealth. This is my number one commitment.

The second commitment is this—I'm a Buddhist. All major religious traditions, in spite different philosophies, have the same potential and also the same message—a message of love, compassion, forgiveness, tolerance, and self-discipline. Therefore, all religious traditions have the same sort of potential to help humanity and bring about these inner human values. Different approaches and philosophies are necessary in order to benefit, influence or impact different kinds of people, because different people have many different dispositions. Just one philosophy is simply not sufficient—we need a variety of philosophies and approaches. It is more useful for a variety of people, as long as the basic aim is the same—try to be a more compassionate and more truthful sort of person. Truthfulness and compassion are the objects of all major religious traditions. Different methods are necessary. Within Buddhism itself, there are different philosophies and different concepts of reality. The Buddha himself preached different contradictory philosophies. Why? Because among his own followers, there were different people and many different dispositions. Just one philosophical view was not sufficient for the variety of people. So obviously we needed different ways of approach. But these differences are only superficial. The essence is the same—to bring inner peace. Therefore, there is a common ground and a common goal, which can be used to try and bring about a closer relationship between different religious traditions. So this is my number two commitment—to promote harmony among different religious traditions.

So that's almost an introduction to myself.

3

PEACE AND COMPASSION

Madison, 2008

D ear brothers and sisters, indeed, I am very, very happy and very honored to speak to you. I speak about nothing special, just our common experience. I am here for the seventh time. And on every occasion, the people here show me genuine human feeling and friendship. So that is also, naturally, one reason why I come happily whenever I receive an invitation. So I am very, very happy.

In the meantime, when I see large number of people who have come to listen to my talk, I always make it clear that, firstly, it's perfectly all right to come here out of curiosity. Then maybe, some people come here to watch what the Dalai Lama is saying. That is also perfectly all right, very good. Whenever I talk, particularly about this Tibet issue, I talk truthfully. I talk about justice. So, anyone who wants to know more of what the Dalai Lama is thinking is also most welcome.

But some people also come with the belief that the Dalai Lama has some kind of miraculous power. That kind of attitude is dangerous. I have no special powers—nothing! If I had real miraculous powers, I may not have had to face these problems. But obviously, there are a lot of problems I'm facing—not my individual ones but those which come with the Dalai Lama's name and responsibilities. I am simply an ordinary person. Because of that, I am simply facing some problems, sometimes unnecessary problems at that.

Then, there is another thing. Some people come to see me with the belief that the Dalai Lama has healing powers. That's ridiculous. Of course, firstly, I do not believe in such healing powers. Just to touch someone physically and cure a disease is impossible. If there are people who really have such healing powers, then after this meeting, I want to see them, because you see, here is my little finger. On one occasion when I visited America, I met a Mongolian, with whom I shook hands as usual, but the man never let my poor finger go. So now, as a result, my poor finger is a little damaged. So if there's someone who has real healing power, this is good opportunity to test it.

(*Laughs*) I have nothing special, and my talk is also a common sort of experience.

It is obvious, everybody—whether Easterner or Westerner, or rich or poor, educated or uneducated, believer or nonbeliever—wants a happy life. And even I think everybody wants a happy dream. In our dreams, we want to be happy. I believe the very purpose of our lives—generally speaking from a secular viewpoint—is to have a happy life. If someone has really lost hope, then that very attitude shortens their life span. In the worst case, suicide may also take place. Therefore, although there is no guarantee of happiness or a happy life, we survive on the basis of hope for the better. Hope means something good. Therefore, the basis of our survival is very much based on the hope of finding a happy life.

In order to gain a happy and comfortable life, we generally believe that material facilities are the basis. I think we come from a society or community or generation where material facilities are lacking. So our mental tendency is to seek out other facilities—more money, more money. Or for example, a hungry person's number one concern is food, food, food. But now, it seems that people from families or societies which are materially affluent and have all material facilities are also beginning to experience the limitation of material value. This is quite natural. External, material facilities can only provide comfort on a physical level.

Basically we are social animals. "Social animal" means that each individual's future or well-being depends on a group of people. So that's our very nature. But the individual person is sometimes lost to that concept. The individual becomes more important than the rest of the community. So instead of respect or the attitude that the community is the basis of their future, they simply utilize, exploit and bully others.

And because your own mental attitude is that way, it becomes very possible to get the impression that others also have a similar attitude—that they are only exploiting or taking advantage of you. Through that belief, you automatically develop fear and suspicion, and distance yourself from others. Deep inside, that brings a feeling of loneliness and helplessness. Once you are in such an unhappy mental state, you get frustrated. That brings anger. That destroys your health and your friendships. So this kind of attitude is very much against our basic nature as a social animal. Because of our basic nature as social animals, you must have very close feelings toward the rest of your community. That mental attitude is usually what we call affection or compassion.

If you extend your genuine sense of concern with respect, that brings genuine friendship and trust. At the communal level, a healthy community means people have to trust each other. It's the basis. Fear and suspicion are the opposite of trust. Where there are fear and suspicion, trust is impossible. Where there is trust, fear and suspicion have no room. So a happy family can be built on the basis of trust and affection. A happy community can develop on the basis of trust and affection. If affection is there, trust comes. Therefore, people gradually seem to be realizing the importance of certain mental values.

Medically speaking, also, warm-heartedness and a compassionate mind bring you better health. Constant fear, anger, or hatred is very bad for our health. Some scientists once told me anger, hatred, and fear are actually eating into our immune systems. Even if you have all the material facility and are resting on a comfortable bed, if you are full of fear or anger, your immune system gets reduced. On the other hand, if you have just poor facilities but are full of confidence, happiness, and good cheer, then your immune system is maintained well. So our physical health is also very much related our mental attitude.

I often mention a particular research undertaken by a group of scientists, where they took some young monkeys, and put a few of them with their mothers and a few of them away from their mothers. The young monkeys who were with their mothers were always playful and happy; they rarely quarrelled. But the young monkeys separated from their mothers were always in a bad mood and often quarrelled. It is the same with us human beings. Those who have lacked affection from their families as children have really difficult lives. Their education suffers because of too much unhappiness. Their physical growth also suffers—this is very clear. But the worst thing is that, for the rest of their lives, they find it difficult to show affection to others. These people often become angry and frustrated people. The frustration transforms to anger, the anger transforms to violence.

Then how can we develop a happy society? Through law, through money alone? A happy society must be created from within. A community or a society means a combination of people, so I think firstly, we must create happy families. Then ten families, a hundred families, a thousand families, like that—and then a happy community can develop.

Even then, there will be a few individual troublemakers. These people can be isolated, so that they cannot influence the happiness, trust, and genuine friendship in the rest of society. In order to create a happy and compassionate family, firstly, compassion must start from the individual. So when we talk about a happier and more peaceful world, I believe the first initiative must come from one individual. Of course, many individuals know that. So each of us has some small potential to create a happy world.

One's own individual future and happiness depends on the rest of the world. Now for example, take my own case—I'm one individual human being, only one among six billion human beings. So much of my future depends on the well-being of the six billion human beings. If the rest of the human beings are facing difficulties, then there will be more violence, and I have to be in constant fear. And with my own peace of mind in danger, it is difficult for me to have a happy life.

Then, particularly in today's world, there is a new reality. The global economies are heavily interdependent. There is the environmental issue. These are universal issues, global issues. So, within this new reality, the concept of one individual or just thinking in terms of "me" and "my generation" is no longer realistic. According to the new reality, the words "we" and "they" are not relevant. The rest of the world is actually a part of you. So, according to that reality, we have to have a sense of concern—a genuine sense of concern for the entire world, for humanity.

Then, there is the subject of world peace. World peace comes automatically through inner peace. If, inside, you are full of hatred, suspicion, and distrust, it is impossible to create peace. So peace must come from the inside.

Hatred, suspicion, distrust—these are violent states of mind. In order to create inner peace, we must have disarmament. Through inner disarmament, there is a real possibility to achieve external disarmament. This is logical. Cause and effect, cause and effect. Every positive or negative human action is related to our emotions and motivations. So therefore, in order to achieve genuine, lasting world peace, firstly, we should take care of our individual inner peace. I think that's important. Now, the most important elements are a sense of concern and responsibility, and a sense of community. These are, I think, key factors.

So now comes the question of compassion or affection. Affection is nothing new to us. The way we are born, immediately after birth we receive maximum affection from our mothers; and with that, we survive. So this body and this life start out in an atmosphere of affection or compassion. That's the way. And, according to medical scientists, after birth, for the next few weeks only the mother's physical touch is necessary for the proper development of the brain of the child. So that's a way that has come not from religion but reality.

One time in Poland, I visited a children's home. Those children, the organizer told me, were "unwanted children." Although there were people feeding or dressing them, of course, and giving them some education and shelter there, I don't think those children's minds were really happy, since their mothers had abandoned them. It is very harmful for the child. So therefore, affection, I think, is a physical product, a biological product. However, if we further analyze, affection or compassion that mainly comes from the biological factor is biased and limited. That kind of biased compassion cannot be extended to a stranger, because his action is neither harmful nor helpful to you—it's neutral. So an affectionate attitude is difficult. Then, particularly with your enemy, because his attitude is harmful to you, there is no basis for compassion. But now, through reasoning that we are social animals—particularly in today's reality where everything is interdependent, from the medical viewpoint also—more compassionate warm-heartedness is good for health.

Then, there is the development of compassion. Anger is bad for your own health, very bad. Also bad for your friendship with your friends. In national relations, in every field, anger and hatred are bad. So one must deliberately try to minimize these negative emotions and deliberately try to increase positive emotions. Then, compassion or affection can be furthered from both.

Now here, it is illogical to say that you should extend compassion toward your enemy because the enemy is harming you. So we have to approach it in a different way. That means, while your enemy is directly harming you, underneath he is also a part of humanity. So your future is also somehow related to him. At least if, because of his attitude, you let yourself get angry toward him, it's bad for your own health. So it is better to keep a positive attitude toward him. Also, in the long run, if you constantly keep affection, today's enemy may one day become your good friend. If you continuously keep your negative attitude, that closes the door to the possibility of becoming friends. Using these sorts of reasons, you can disregard your enemy's attitude.

Now, for example, take my own case. I have a certain amount of compassion. The seed of this has not come from my teacher or Buddhist teaching, but from my mother. My mother was so kind. She was an illiterate village farmer—a village mother—but a very, very warm-hearted person. My mother was so compassionate. At a very young age—one year, two years—as with other children, my mother always carried me around. So then, sometimes, I used to bully my mother. I held my mother's ears. If I wanted to go this way, I would do this. (*Mimes pulling*) If my mother went in a direction which I did not want, then I would cry. I, that young boy, was more aggressive than my mother. Very bad. So my mother was really very kind. I always feel that the seed of my compassion today originally comes from my mother. Everybody has a mother. So therefore, compassion is something important and everybody has the potential for that from birth. The only point is whether we pay more attention and make that effort or not. Otherwise, everybody has the potential. Another aspect of compassion is that a more compassionate attitude means that, deep inside, there is self-confidence. So that means, deep inside, you have strength.

With a lot of anger and hatred, there comes a little bit of uncertainty. Compassion means not just thinking of oneself but taking care of others, considering others. That means you have strength. A self-centered attitude means not thinking of others but only of one's own things—that brings anxiety. So therefore, compassion brings inner strength. Inner strength brings a calm mind. A calm mind is one very important factor for the functioning of our brains. Fear is very bad. Anger as well. As our lives are quite complicated, we need to clearly analyze things. Without knowing the reality, without the help of analysis, you cannot see the reality. Then all your actions become unrealistic.

For example, if some mosquito comes, there's not much need to analyze. If you feel hungry, then no need for analysis—just think of food. So when you're feeling hungry, you don't need to resort to complicated analyses, for example, wondering whether your hunger will be satisfied with the first spoonful or the second or the third, and so on. What particle is this food made of, what is going inside the stomach—no, you don't need these things, just eat the food. But otherwise, you see, for more complicated actions, we need a clear understanding, a clear awareness of the reality of our goals. So, in order to know reality, we need to investigate through various directions or angles. Just one dimension is not sufficient.

One of my scientist friends once told me when you develop anger, the object of your anger appears negative. So, about ninety percent of that negativity is actually mental projection. This has not come from religious texts but from scientists. The Buddhist texts also have mentions like that. If your mind is agitated, you cannot see reality, because agitation comes from only one aspect of the object. There are other aspects to it too.

Now, for example, we lost our own country over fifty years ago. If I look only at that aspect, my sadness increases. But if I can look at the same event from another angle: because we lost our own country, we gained the new opportunity of meeting different people. And particularly me—I have found meeting scientists very helpful. Meeting people from different faiths was also very, very helpful to understand the value of other religious traditions. If I was still in Lhasa—in Potala, which people sometimes call the Golden Cage—then my mind would not have been what it is today, I think. Of course, even today I'm learning some new thing through personal contact, on a day-to-day basis.

And many Tibetans—at least 150,000 Tibetans—gained this new opportunity with me, of learning new things and making more friends. And it was also helpful, to increase awareness about Tibetan culture. So this negative event brought a lot of positive things. So look from different angles. There's not much need for much sadness. Ah, there are possible things also there. Your enemy—if you look at one particular action, you feel frustration and anger. But if you look from a different angle, he is not that bad. If you make comparison, another one is even worse. Then this event may be more acceptable. Look at one event from different angles and different dimensions. One dimension, four dimensions, six dimensions. *Then* you get the clearer picture about the reality. So to carry such investigations, a normal and calm mind is very important. An agitated mind cannot carry that kind of function right. So from that viewpoint also, the compassionate mind is something important and valuable. I think that is about the power of compassion. What do you think, does it make some sense? (*Laughs*)

So this is what I usually call secular values. Nothing to do with religion. And the way of approach is also nothing to do with religion. But simply, use our common sense, common experience, and scientific findings. Of course, the theistic religious believers use the concept of God to promote these things. And non-theistic religious behavior, the law of causality, uses that concept and promotes compassion. All major religious traditions carry the same message. Message of love, compassion, forgiveness in spite different philosophy. So that's my number two commitment—the promotion of religious harmony.

Above all is emotional human value. As I mentioned earlier, through a secular way of approach. So if you have some interest then investigate further, contemplate further, and then try to implement. Then you get some experience. If you feel it is something good, something useful, then carry further, practice. If you feel there is not much value, benefit, then forget it, no problem.

So, thank you, that's my talk, now questions.

QUESTIONS

QUESTION: *When our negative mind is so strong that we are unable to apply the antidotes, what do we do?*

HIS HOLINESS: I think with negative emotions such as anger or fear, there are two kinds. Some fear is reasonable and helpful and some fear is unnecessary. So basically, I think hatred produces a very negative feeling. Otherwise anger also can be positive and negative, as well as egoistic attitude.

As I mentioned earlier, in negative fear and constant anger or too much attachment, during that moment the implementation of antidote is difficult. So there must be some kind of neutral state. I think one easiest method is to just forget the object about which we feel negative things, forget that, just concentrate on breathing, take out, in out, in out, just meditate on breathing. Twenty times, thirty, forty, one hundred times. Then afterward your mind little bit calmer. Then maybe easier to contemplate, to apply the antidotes. For the moment, don't think both sides, meditate on breathing. Then after some time your mind will be calmer, then think about the positive sides. Try that. That's one method.

Then basically like our immune system, our basic attitude is important. If our basic attitude is more compassionate, and then certain agitations come and go, and there is not much effect. So if your basic attitude is poor, it is not easy to tackle these things. In order to develop positive basic attitude, firstly we need knowledge. Then secondly, constant effort. Then thirdly, time factor. Constant effort with fuller knowledge. Weeks or months may not give a positive result. Years could be needed. Then your main mental attitude can transform. So we need patience. And some of our practitioners, some people want to change quickly. That's unrealistic to one's expectations. It's unrealistic. Take time. Shaping our mind takes time. Not easy. Next question.

QUESTION: *What is the source of your strength and endurance in the face of offences?*

HIS HOLINESS: Good sleep! Good food! (*Laughs*) Then, of course, what I call analytical meditation. Ah, there are some problems. As Shantideva stated, I recite daily sentences: "When faced with tragedy, think. Then when there is way to overcome that tragedy, then no need to worry, make effort to work on that. If there is no way to overcome the tragedy, then no use to worry. Accept." As a Buddhist, blame karma. Accept. If you believe in God, to some extent, with respect, blame God.

QUESTION: *What is the most useful method of acquiring virtuous qualities, to encourage people of all types, individually or in groups, to forgive previous mistakes and harbor no ill will toward others?*

HIS HOLINESS: I think forgiveness may be related with accepting reality. Something happens. Some bad things happen. Accept that. Then if others have done something, forgive. No use in holding on to ill feeling. Forgiveness does not mean to forget. Or forgiveness does not mean you accept the other's wrongdoing. I think the essence of forgiveness is not to have negative feelings such as anger arise toward the wrongdoer. Forgiveness does not mean you accept others' wrongdoing. Now as far as wrongdoing is concerned, in some cases you need countermeasures in order to stop that. But the countermeasure should be carried out of a sense of concern for the wrongdoer. If one lets the wrongdoer do wrong continuously, its harmful for them. So out of a sense of concern, out sense of compassion, stop them. Try to stop. Utilize certain countermeasures. That's, I think, really not letting anger out, out of a sense of concern, compassion. That's true sense of forgiveness. You see, sometimes people get the impression that the practice of compassion involves some kind of foolishness, unable to distinguish between right and wrong. Or indifference. That's not the case.

QUESTION: *It is amazing that the Tibetans have still enough identity to revolt against the Chinese authorities as they did earlier this year. Can you tell us what you know of the status of Tibetans in Tibet in terms of their national identity, and the vitality of the survival of Buddhism, the strength of Buddhism, among them?*

HIS HOLINESS: I think every human community's identity is very much related to its culture and cultural heritage. A Chinese professor who came from mainland China and was very unbiased and honest once described, "Tibetan culture is stronger than Chinese culture." He observed that.

For example, China has very recently opened itself up to the outside world, and now already, a lot of young Chinese are rushing to copy the Western culture. Including culture here. (*Points to his head*) You can see this among the Japanese also. I think among the Indians, very few people dye their hair. Of course, some actors need to dye the color of hair for the film they're shooting; but otherwise very few people dye their hair in India.

I think generally—of course I'm not expert in these things—that we need to do more research. Since India was part of the British imperialist colony, the Indian people's English education is very good, but they have also retained their own culture. Among Tibetans, I have seen few who have dyed their hair in different colors. But Tibetans, generally, also have long tradition of useful culture. I think that gives them some kind of inner strength. Buddhism has also certainly helped. I often express the desire that someone should carry out research to determine the mental state of refugees—refugees from Tibet, from Shinjang near Bangladesh, and also from other Buddhist countries like Cambodia and Vietnam. What's the difference in their mental levels? I have met some refugees from Shinjang who are in their early sixties. Their attitude and the Tibetan attitude toward the Chinese are a little different.

I think this must be because of a difference in compassion. We Tibetans pray and we pray for "all," by which we mean all sentient beings. That means including our Chinese brothers and sisters. Due to recent government propaganda, many Chinese people get the feeling that we Tibetans are anti-Chinese. Absolutely not. We Tibetans respect the Chinese people very much—as a cultured, hardworking, and practical people. Wherever the Chinese people live, they eventually create a Chinatown, with the Chinese language, Chinese scripts, and certainly with good Chinese food, delicious food! So you see, they are a hardworking and cultured people. But then, because of the government propaganda, they have turned very much against Tibet. And that's very bad, very sad. So I want to make this clear—we always respect the Chinese people, but we don't respect the Chinese government and its totalitarian regime. Everybody knows human beings by nature love freedom. Totalitarianism is an obstacle to freedom. So please don't misunderstand our resistance to the dictators' stubbornness. It should not be considered anti-Chinese activity, please.

QUESTION: *Other religions talk about the beginning and end of the world. What does the Buddha say about this?*

HIS HOLINESS: Not only the Buddha but also Mahavira, the Jain teacher, the teacher of Jainism, as far as I know, both believe in the law of causality. So law of causality means that a certain event takes place due to its own causes. That cause is also due to its own causes. So from that way, the cause of another event is actually an event, of its own cause.

Now for example, the Big Bang. It any way is the beginning of this new universe. But the Big Bang must have its own causes and conditions. But obviously tremendous energy, dense energy that caused the Big Bang. So where that energy comes from, what is the cause and condition. So go to the beginning place.

Then another aspect is the physical level. Another aspect is being a self. One self. No independent self. Self is designated on the combination of body and mind. As I mentioned earlier, ultimate particles of this body come from parent to parent to parent to parent. And so it goes, the beginning of the world, before that, empty space, there are particles; even the subtlest particles are a cause of the later development. So today's mind–body is the ultimate continuation of mind–body's particles related with previous time. So it is beginningless. Similarly, the mind is a different phenomenon. It has no shape, no color, no form. So all the time it is changing. That means there must be causes.

Buddhists say there is no beginning of the self, because there is no beginning of consciousness. If you accept beginning of consciousness, then that original consciousness must come from different types of phenomena. That's illogical. That's the basis of previous lives, and rebirth. If you feel uncomfortable, then forget it. Don't think. Now end, within Buddhism, within Buddhist tradition, there are two types. One say, after Buddha's stage, a higher stage, one's body disappears. But most of the Buddhist tradition rejects that. There's no reason to cease our consciousness. So therefore, consciousness still remains to highest spiritual state. So from the Buddhist viewpoint, consciousness is beginningless and endingless.

QUESTION: *What is my life's purpose and more specifically, how should my life purpose best be served in terms of a future career and my ability to link my livelihood with my spiritual development? For example, right now, I work in corporate America, in business, and make an excellent living but feel unfulfilled and somewhat trapped. Although I know this is my own creation, will becoming a healthcare provider or nurse for the dying be a better fit for me in this life? This will mean going back to school and earning less money. In short, what is my next step in realizing, and forwarding, my next life?*

HIS HOLINESS: I appreciate your sincere question. Very good. I think basically as I mentioned before, there are external values, material values, and mental values or internal values. I think we should go for internal values. So I fully agree. Serving, teachers, nurses, this is something directly helping, serving. These are usually what I call compassionate actions. Wonderful. But if all people were involved in nursing or teaching, then from where will the money come?

We should have businessmen. We should have these corporate people. And I think experienced, wise people are very necessary in this field. Otherwise, the corporate world will collapse. So human society needs a variety of people and professions. But here, every human action, whether destructive or constructive, ultimately depends on motivation.

Make money, not from self-centered motivation or discontent about your own lavish lifestyle, but to also think about the world and poor people. There are a lot of needy people there in Africa. People, many people, are facing starvation. Same people. Same human beings. They also have the right to survive. Not only survive but happily. We need money. Then the question is how to utilize the money.

Just to have a personal, lavish lifestyle is I think morally wrong. But we also need money. And to spend wisely. This gap, between the rich and the poor is very, very bad. Here, in the United States, now, the richer billionaires are increasing. Poor people are still poor, sometimes getting poorer. It is a shame, it's bad. So, we need money to reduce this sort of gap, and provide equipment and expertise through education. Then the poorer sections, instead of having frustration and anger, work hard for education, for training, based on self-confidence. We are the same human people, taking care of each other, we must work hard, and we must train. So I think we need money. I think we ought to work. Carry on with sincere motivation and a global sort of view. I think it's very possible. That is also compassionate work. Constructive work. Very good.

QUESTION: *I am thirty-nine years old. I am a widow. My husband died after a long battle with drugs and alcohol. He overdosed at only thirty-six years of age. I need to find my own inner peace. I struggle with this every day. Can you suggest some ways I can help to center myself to help me find a path through this pain and anguish? I love life, and I like feeling happy. But I miss having these emotions. My heart is heavy, and my mind hurts. Can you please offer me any advice? Thank you.*

HIS HOLINESS: Very sad. Sad story. I don't know. As I mentioned, in my own practice, I have also experienced tragedy. That has already happened. Now I think one thing, if you worry, worry, worry, you remain like that. If your late husband really loved you, and, I think, your parents really love you, so in some way they know about your mental state today.

If your mind, mental state in spite of this tragedy, tries to be calm and carry your work normally, I think your parents and also your late husband, must feel happy. If you remain with this kind of very sad state, in some way, knowing this your parents and your friends will also feel very sad. So tragedy already happened. Now I think this tragedy should transform your self-confidence and bring more energy, your life should be something useful for society, for the community. And through that way, you gain more self-confidence and joyfulness. If you remain sad, sad, sad, then there is no possibility to gain self-confidence.

So work hard. And that tragedy, sadness, should transform into new energy. Work hard. And your own tragic case, in six billion human beings, such things plenty. Not just your own case. So that's also you see, I think, helpful. Sometimes some tragedy happens, and then your first reaction is "Oh, how bad I have this kind of experience." Then think, "Oh, among six billion, there are many others who also have this same experience, is some cases even worse." That also, sometimes is helpful, to reduce your unbearable feeling. Then if you believe in God, then think of God. If this is tragedy, then deeper level, there must be some meaning. That is also helpful. If you're not a believer, then use common sense as I mentioned before. If discussion lead to some sort of knowledge or interest in God, non-theistic religion, then think of the law of causality. Every event, every experience takes place due to its own cause and conditions. So mainly these causes are one's own creation. Certain consequences fail today because of certain previous actions. That is also helpful.

So thank you.

Part Five

NON-VIOLENCE
AND SECULAR
ETHICS

1

ETHICS FOR THE NEW MILLENNIUM

Goa, 2011

I have passed through Goa several times as there is a Tibetan settlement nearby, but it is the first time I am here for a meeting. The Chief Minister could arrange a meeting and I would like to thank him for this great honor.

By nature, every human being innately wants happiness and doesn't want suffering. Even animals or insects have the same desire. Everybody has the right to lead a happy life, overcome problems, and pursue happiness. Now, the word "happiness" does not mean just satisfaction but a deeper, mental-level satisfaction. It is important to make a distinction between the satisfaction that comes through sensorial feeling and deeper satisfaction.

Sensorial satisfaction can be obtained by looking at something pleasing to the eyes or listening to some music. This kind of mental satisfaction depends on external matters but they are not permanent in nature. Once they disappear, the mental satisfaction reduces and what is left is a memory. The other level of satisfaction—deep satisfaction—only comes through leading a meaningful life and saving other people. All those people who have faith in God and meditate can attain inner satisfaction and they are not dependent on external factors. Deep satisfaction attained out of meditation is more durable. In case of sensorial satisfaction, when the source of satisfaction is removed or when people reach an old age and their senses are weak, then sensorial satisfaction becomes difficult to attain, especially if they have no experience of deep mental satisfaction.

Not understanding the deeper level of satisfaction and depending only on money and wealth does not guarantee happiness. If a rich person owns an expensive ring, no matter how much he kisses it, the ring will not respond. On the other hand, if the same affection is showed to animals, they will respond in kind and that will make the person happy. Genuine affection, when shown, gets an equal response and that makes a person and the family happy. Wealth may bring extreme suspicion and competition. It becomes impossible to develop a genuine friendship in the midst of suspicion and destructive competition.

Money has to be used wisely—otherwise material value diminishes human value. I tell my businessmen friends that they are the slaves of money. Often I notice that they are not happy and suffer from too much stress and anxiety. I am not opposed to development, because we do have the physical body and taking care of it is highly necessary. With the help of technology and science, we have come long a way, but we cannot depend on them for the peace and happiness of the people, as they have also become destructive forces. In the twentieth century, over two hundred million people have been killed through violence. As destructive powers have increased in the world, the casualties have increased significantly too.

A person should not neglect inner values, as they are very important. I lost my freedom at the age of sixteen, and at the age of twenty-four, I lost my country. All Tibetan people have put their trust in me and it's my moral responsibility, but the situation is helpless. (*Laughs*) I do not consume any form of tranquilizer. As a Buddhist, I am not supposed to consume them. But even though I am heartbroken, though not for long, I still don't take any alcohol or drugs. I can keep my mind calm and thus I am relatively happy. All human beings are born with the same potential to achieve, but they develop with knowledge, a calm mind and warm-heartedness, with the parents' affection.

In order to develop inner human values, I feel that there are three ways. Firstly, religious faith or faith in God helps a person to gain compassion, a sense of tolerance and patience, and a certain discipline, which ultimately promotes inner values. Even for the believers of non-idolatrous religions like Jainism and Buddhism, the people believe that there is no creator but ultimately self-creation. They believe in theories like Darwin's, which states that the world is made of atoms and as the components gather together they create different individuals. Indians, on the other hand, believe in karma, which means that everything happens in response to one's own actions. Any action that brings happiness to others results in your happiness, and similarly, any action that brings harm to others—like murder, rape and lies—brings forth negative consequences. Thus, in order to attain happiness, you have to serve others and not harm others.

Thirdly, some Christian and Muslim friends of mine believe that ethics are based on morals, but I believe the basis of ethics is compassion. Even animals have ethics. For example, if you are kind to a dog, he will respond in kind and be loyal to you. A child, as soon as it is born, is dependent on its mother for affection. Thus, ethics should be without any influence from religion. In case of India, to avoid any complications, the forefathers like Gandhi and Rajendra Prasad adopted secularism. Secularism. as opposed to the popular belief. is not disrespecting any religion but respecting all religions equally. India has a huge population of nonbelievers, too, and the Indian constitution respects them too.

Human values can be promoted among believers and nonbelievers by using three common experiences:

i) Growing up with the mother's affection from a very young age usually helps a person to be stable in life. Lack of a mother's care sows the seeds of insecurity and leads to an unstable life.

ii) Community and family play a very important role, too. If the community or family live with compassion in their lives, they are able to tackle any problem that comes their way. Rich, influential families—even the ones with a lot of money and power—can be very depressed. One has to realize the importance of affectionate attitude, as it leads to a calm mind and ultimately a healthy person. Anyone living without affection in their lives will have deep-seated insecurities and anxieties.

iii) Until the later part of twentieth century, science did not pay much attention to the importance of the inner world or the mind. Later, with developments in the field of medical science or neuron science, the scientists realized that the inner world is an important factor for health.

In the last thirty years, I have met and discussed with scientists on this issue. Many of them carry out experiments on groups of people. Before initiating them into a program designed to learn and incorporate compassion and affection in life, the doctors check their blood pressure, amount of stress, and so forth. After two weeks into the program, the doctors again checked these things and discovered that blood pressure and stress have reduced considerably.

I visited an American university which carried out similar experiments on its students and found out that their concentration, sharpness, and social conduct had improved, because of which they became much happier. Medical scientists have stated that fear eats away our immune systems, and calm-minded people fall less ill and recover faster too. On one occasion, a doctor conducted an experiment with two injured guinea pigs. One of the injured guinea pigs was kept in isolation and another one was kept with a companion. The one with the companion recovered faster.

A scientist from Columbia University stated that people who say "I," "my" and "me" quite often have a greater chance of heart attack. From that I understood that self-centered people don't have a calm mind and, thus, they find even a small problem unbearable. But if the person thinks in a more holistic manner, even a big problem can be dealt with a calm mind.

Human beings are social animals by nature and thus community is the basis of a happy life. Trust can be gained only if one possesses a genuine sense of concern; through trust comes cooperation, and friendship comes from cooperation, which leads to a peaceful existence. The foundation for the ultimate peace comes from education and reasoning, not religion.

We had a meeting in Delhi with spiritual masters and scientists about the importance of warm-heartedness and discussed issues like introducing elementary-level children to warm-heartedness in a secular way, in order to reduce the emphasis on appearance and know the reality. That way, we can help the youth to inculcate qualities like conviction and warm-heartedness. Usually, as I have explained before, we are selfish by nature and thus we don't manage to develop compassion toward each other. But compassion is an extension of self-love and thus one can be extremely happy if they bring happiness to others. Narrow-sighted love can only lead to self-destruction. That is what I mean by the secular way of compassion.

QUESTIONS

QUESTION: *I would like to know what the purpose of life is and whether you believe in destiny. If yes, then what is the role of destiny in life?*

HIS HOLINESS: According to the Buddhist point of view (though my own viewpoint differs from it), the eyes, the mind, and the desire to overcome something are all part of nature. I think secularly, that's the answer. The very purpose of life, I believe, is happiness. There is no guarantee in life but we survive because of hope. If we lose our hope then that will shorten our lives. Our survival is based on the hope for a good future, not a bad future. From this point of view, happiness is the sole purpose of life.

Destiny is fixed and we have no power to change it, according to different faiths. But according to the secular path, there is no destiny. Events occur due to causes and conditions; for example, an unhealthy body will lead to weakened destiny. If the body is cared for, then destiny can change. Thus, destiny can change if there is effort put into it.

QUESTION: *Can you please tell us how to overcome hatred and fear? And can you throw some light on Zen?*

HIS HOLINESS: There are many levels of hatred and it can be described as an ill-feeling toward the troublemaker, the enemy, or the friend. But anger is a part of our emotions, which erupts as a defense mechanism in a person when he/she encounters negative situation or danger. Biologically speaking, emotions like anger, desire, and attachment are necessary for survival. Hatred can be described as the residue of the anger which remains and festers for a long time.

I don't have hatred, but if I see something that is wrong, I become angry. After the crisis in Tibet on March 10, 2008, I felt the same emotions that I felt on March 10, 1959, when I lost freedom—helplessness, hopelessness, fear, and anxiety. Yet, the emotions did differ, as after the 2008 crisis, I visualized the Chinese officials and I exchanged their fear and anger for my patience and compassion. Obviously, it did not solve any problems, but it helped me in maintaining my mental peace.

One can simply pray to eliminate hatred. According to Buddhist psychology, dealing with negative emotions is important. The hatred which is about to develop has to be dealt with initially. Irritation acts as a catalyst for anger to develop into hatred. At that point, one needs to remember that anger is not a solution but only helps in the destruction of happiness. That will help in reducing the unpleasant thoughts forming in the mind.

The condition of the body also matters, as a weak body may cause serious negativity, but a healthy body will result in a strong mind which won't be disturbed easily. Through practice, one needs to learn to separate the self from anger, which will make one look at the anger logically and ultimately vanquish it altogether. If the anger spreads throughout the mind, it becomes difficult to remove. Buddhist psychology and Hindu psychology have elements like Vipassana and Samadhi which explain the methods to tackle the mind.

When I pass through small towns in India, I find Hindu temples like those of the Shiva lingam, Vishnu temples, Ganesh temples—I wonder, why not construct more places where the followers can sit and discuss the scriptures rather than temples that just house a single statue of a deity? I have often told the Tibetans to not to construct more Buddha statues. I am Buddhist but I know that the Buddha statue will never speak; thus it's better to print more books which will prove to be more beneficial. The scriptures have been there for the last three thousand years, but what is lacking is the study of them. Many Indians are very faithful followers of religion, but they do not pay attention to the study of the scriptures.

QUESTION: *Doctors universally have to take the Hippocratic Oath before they can start their practice of medicine. Is there a public oath you suggest which the politicians should adopt universally?*

HIS HOLINESS: I am not a politician. Many years ago, the parliament in Delhi constructed Gandhi's statue. I was invited for the opening ceremony and I told the politicians to remember Gandhi's truthfulness every time they passed by the statue. During India's freedom fight, all the leaders were selfless, fearless, and honest with their work. I have often told my Indian friends that in the last sixty years since their freedom, leaders need the same spirit like the freedom fighters. They too need to be honest, truthful, and selfless.

India is a democratic country and has an independent judiciary, which makes it a peaceful country. At a meeting which was attended by many judges and lawyers, I teased them while praising them that if the people who deliver justice are a little dishonest, then it becomes a real disaster. India is a huge country, thus the small things that take place occasionally are understandable. But it is much more stable than the neighboring states.

The media in India has a really important role to play. In a democratic country, their role attains more importance as they have the responsibility of educating the people about the events taking place around them. Thus, they need to maintain the basic human values, secular ethics, and religious harmony. Along with that, they need to make sure that they communicate the truths about politicians, social workers, media, and businessmen, but making sure that they are not presenting any convoluted facts to the people. In China, due to the lack of an independent media, the system experiences a lot of corruption, which the rich and powerful people are free to exploit. The media should investigate the world thoroughly and let people know facts in an unbiased manner.

QUESTION: *You said that money does not give happiness—I agree. But I believe that money can buy things to make your life comfortable. So, according to Buddhist psychology, can you suggest a way which draws a balance between acquiring wealth and making you happy?*

HIS HOLINESS: We have this body and to make it comfortable we need food and shelter. I pass through villages with very poor people who have never experienced this comfort. Globally, the gap between the rich and the poor is huge. Attention should be paid to bridge the gap on the global and the national levels. India's economy grows quite well, and it is a liberal society, unlike China. Thus, it is a healthy society. Real transformation should take place in rural India with more attention paid to rural development.

I do agree that the money is important. Blessings are not sufficient. Hard work is important too. Actual transformation comes from hard work and not just praying. Rich people should give poor people education and technical skills. A few days ago I was in a town which I had visited two decades ago, when the locals had expressed their decision of developing. I promised them Rs 10 crore as a donation and the state promised funds too. When I went there recently, the people had developed some skills and were living quite peacefully.

Now, has any one of you experienced some swings between happy mood and bad mood? When you are sad and have money in your pockets, can you go to a big shop and demand for a peaceful mind? Or can you visit a big hospital for a peaceful-mind injection, or ask for an inner-peace technology from a factory? Only if they keep your brain aside and replace it with some mechanical thing will you be indifferent and not experience any feelings. Do you really want that?

Therefore, it's obvious that money is needed only for physical needs, not for mental peace. We need both the body and the mind to be healthy. Thus, buy the material facilities but don't worship the money. Realize that there is a limitation on economic value, and summon your energy to attain inner peace.

QUESTION: *It has seemed over last the few months that there are worrying signs in the media over the lama who had some funds. It seems that your presence and the presence of the large Tibetan community in India are starting to be a kind of an inconvenience in India's vision of global rise. Do you have some concerns about the future of your community and the stability of your relationship with India which has existed for so long?*

HIS HOLINESS: The relation between Tibet and India has not existed for a few decades but thousands of years. I have always maintained that our relationship is like the relationship between a guru and his chela—India is the guru and we are the chela. For example, during the seventh or eighth century, Buddhism entered Tibet and flourished and changed the way of living. Now the Indian civilization and the Tibetan civilization—like Morarji Desai said in reply to the congratulatory note which I wrote to him when he became the Prime Minister of India—are like branches of one bodhi tree. That tree grew in India and extended toward Tibet. We have a very strong relationship.

Tibet is controlled by Chinese communists, but in their mind they are looking at this country. In 1956, the Indian government invited me and I reached here with great difficulty. Since then I developed a very special relationship with Nehru and Rajendra Prasad. In 1959, India gave me and my people political asylum. They helped in starting Tibetan schools and resettlements, especially in states of Himachal Pradesh and Karnataka. After fifty-one years, my community is well settled here. That's the kind of relationship we share with this country.

Geographically, India shares a border with Tibet. No Indian soldier was ever seen across a thousand miles of this border. After 1959, and especially after 1962, military posts were built. The issue of Tibet is an issue for India too. Small misunderstandings are always there. Some misunderstandings crept up due to the carelessness of a worker, but otherwise there is nothing serious about the lama issue.

QUESTION: *Is it silly to think that religion can become a cause for a war? In that case, does religion become a friend of peace or war? Would there be more peace if it were abolished?*

HIS HOLINESS: War for religion is a part of human history. Some people do believe that it will be better if there is no religion, but then the First World War, the Second World War or the Korean War did not take place because of religious issues. Some conflict is always there. In the past, some conflicts have occurred because of religion. Yet, I believe that the name of religion is misused for power.

Religion is used to manipulate people. The religious people are too attached to their own religions. In Argentina, at a meeting with scientists and religious leaders, a Chilean scientist told me that he thought he should not be too attached even to his scientific field. Even I should not develop attachment to Buddhism, because a biased mind cannot see reality. Any religious follower with too much attachment to their religion becomes a fanatic, which is a mistake.

Many Hindus believe in Krishna and Shiva, but when I ask them to define Hinduism, they don't have an answer. I tease my friends who chant some Sanskrit shlokas in the morning but don't know what they mean. They keep flowers at the feet of Ganesha or any other idol, but have no idea why they need to do that. I think many Muslims say Allah's name but don't know what it means. My friend says that if any Muslim sheds another person's blood, then he does not remain a Muslim. One should have love and compassion for other beings, only then he can be called a genuine practitioner of Islam. The meaning of jihad is defined by the Muslims from terrorist cells who don't know the real teaching of the Koran. They develop an attachment to their religion and become fanatics.

Even among the Buddhists, there are fanatics. They don't like my way of teaching and are against me because my approach does not conform with traditional Buddhist teachings. The best situation will be if the six billion people should disappear and only then genuine world peace can be attained. One should pray to God to make the entire human civilization vanish. Jokes apart, one should stay and cultivate infinite compassion. Humans need to develop further and should know the reality and their own ability.

2

Non-Violence and Spiritual Values in Secular India

New Delhi, 2011

I have a clear memory of President Venkataraman's genuine sense of concern and keen interest about both Tibetan culture and Buddhism. He was really a wonderful person—a former president of this great country but very humble and simple. I recall the first Indian president, Rajendra Prasad, who was also like that. I feel very happy.

There is one secret I want to share with you. In 1954, Pandit Nehru came to Peking for a banquet or something. I was introduced to Pandit Nehru with all the other leaders. Besides myself, Zhou Enlai and the Pancham Lama were also there. So then, I was introduced as the Dalai Lama. Pandit Nehru remained motionless. I thought at that moment he reflected on all the effects of Tibet.

Zhou Enlai was very smart and immediately introduced the next person. Pandit Nehru, a great leader and an experienced person, felt such a strong emotion that he remained standing like that. I also felt a little embarrassed.

Of course, for the 1956 Buddha Jayanti celebration I had several meetings with Nehru, and sometimes a little bit of heated discussion also, because at that time, you know, my officials and my two brothers very much insisted I should remain in India. I discussed with Pandit Nehru, and he advised me to go back. And one day he came to see me at Hyderabad House where I was staying. He brought a copy of the 17-Point Agreement and showed it to me. So really he showed concern.

We had several meetings after that. Sometimes when I entered through his gate I was a little nervous, but after many meetings, it became a very close feeling. He was very nice person. And I also learned what democracy was—freedom of speech and freedom of expression. At some points, when we requested a lot for Tibetan issues, he disagreed. But we'd decided our own way. After that when I met him, I hesitated a little—What would his reaction be? But he was completely normal. I learned that that was the meaning of freedom of expression and different thought, and that he understood that. In China, it's not like that. (*Laughs*) I learned that through nine years spent daily with Chinese leaders. Of course, Chairman Mao was quite exceptional. But then later I found his nice promise was not very sincere, not implemented later. So that means a word is only word, but action is another thing.

Anyway, I am extremely happy to come here. As soon as I entered, I reflected on those years of my experience. You see, Tibetans pronounce Jawaharlal as "Jhwala." "Jhwala" in our language means elder brother. So Nehru is our elder brother—Jhwala Nehru, Jhwala Nehru. And then I want to thank our music conductor. I usually I don't have much interest in things like music, but the way you conducted it was very lively, full of involvement—that kind of thing. I appreciate it, thank you.

Now, I talk about non-violence and spiritual values in a secular India. I think there is hardly anything to say to Indian brothers and sisters. (*Laughs*) You already know these things for more than two thousand years. However, the younger generation is only interested in technology, science, and computers, so maybe it is worthwhile to remind them of their tradition, which exists and develops in this country and has been maintained for more than two thousand years.

Firstly, non-violence. What is non-violence? We cannot make a real demarcation between violence and non-violence from apparent action, but have to search for a deeper motivation. For example, a good teacher or parent, when dealing with a naughty student or child, will sometimes show a little tough or harsh attitude, but out of genuine sense of concern for their future well-being. Actually, because that action is carried out of a genuine sense of concern or compassion, that's essentially non-violence. On the other hand, when the motivation to cheat or exploit another is disguised by talking nicely or a smile, that action is artificial, that smile is not a genuine smile. You receive that person with a smile, praise him, or give him some gift—all this non-violence. But because his ultimate motivation is to cheat, harm, deceive, or exploit, it is a violent action. So ultimately, non-violence is very much related to motivation.

I usually say that non-violence is an act of compassion. With a genuine sense of concern for others' well-being—no matter how difficult it is—you must treat them as human brothers and sisters, and realize that they also have the right to overcome suffering. Understanding that and avoiding force or violence is true non-violence. Now, the helpless way—not harming others—is not non-violence. That's not a choice. Real non-violence is when you have the opportunity or the ability, but deliberately restrain violence out of a sense of compassion. That is real non-violence.

Now about spirituality and spiritual values, in spite of differences in philosophical views, all major religious institutions carry the same message of love, compassion, forgiveness, tolerance, and also of contentment and self-discipline. These are the elements of genuine non-violent motivation. In the secular way, like in this country, it also includes nonbelievers. I think of secularism according to the Indian view. Secularism does not at all disrespect religion, but respects all religions, with no preference for this or that religion. All religions are respected.

Some of my friends—some Muslims and Christians—have a little reservation about word "secularism." But according to India, secularism is not at all disrespect or some kind of negative rejection. For more than three thousand years, this country developed different religions, views, and believers. One ancient tradition is the Sankhya philosophy, which has existed even before Buddha. A lot of subdivisions developed from the Sankhya philosophy. Then Buddhism and Jainism developed as well.

Then, of course, from the outside, Zoroastrianism came, followed by Christianity and Islam, also Judaism, and then later Sikhism. And because of the circumstances, Guru Nanak respected both the Muslims and the Hindus and all other traditions. So Sikhism is a kind of non-sectarian religion. Because of that reality, for a thousand years, Indians basically have had a very open mind. From childhood, they already know about all the different kinds of religions.

I see in Kerala, at the grassroots, this tradition has been kept for a thousand years. So, secularism respects all religions, and then, as I mentioned earlier, there is also the nonbeliever. I think that's really the strength of India. And usually, I describe India as our guru, we are their chela. I myself carry two of India's traditions—non-violence or ahimsa, and religious harmony. Wherever I go, I always talk about these two things. So I consider myself as a messenger of ancient Indian thought. So I'm often saying, "At the messenger level, I'm quite active to promote these things. Now my real boss should take a more active role regarding the promotion of non-violence and religious harmony. The world needs that."

These two things—non-violence and religious harmony—are not only ancient but very relevant to today's world. Look among

Christians—they believe in the same Trinity—but Catholics and Protestants are fighting in Northern Ireland. Very sad. I have been to Northern Ireland on a few occasions. Again, you see, both the Sunni and the Shia sects follow the teachings of the same Prophet Muhammad and use the same Koran. But due to small differences here and there, they are fighting and killing each other. Very sad.

So sometimes, also, religion also becomes a factor of division. All religions talk of love, compassion, and a sense of brotherhood and sisterhood. Particularly the theistic religions preach that all people come from the same source. So according to that view, they are truly brothers and sisters. But these really wise and orthodox views are neglected and there is too much emphasis on the small things, which lead to fighting.

So for thousands of years you've kept these two things still very much alive in this country. Now you must show them to the rest of the world—wherever there is conflict or division in the name of religion. Now you must take an active role in this field, not for political or economic reasons but simply for the sake of human beings. Secularism has a high emphasis on secular ethics, because in reality, a large section of now seven billion human beings is not serious about religion.

This is also an important part of humanity. Whether they believe in religion or not, that's an individual's business. But they must be good, compassionate citizens. I mean compassionate human beings are part of humanity. That's very important. So if we say, "Oh, the practice of love and compassion is something important because the Buddha said so, or Jesus Christ said so, or Mohammad said so," then these people say, "Oh, I don't care. I have no interest in these things." So we must have ways and means to bring conviction to these people. The practice of compassion, loving and kindness is for your own well-being.

Everybody wants happiness and good health. Medicine alone may not bring good health. Now medical doctors and scientists have begun to realize that peace and calmness of mind is the key factor for good health. And the calmer the mind, the more peaceful the mind, comes more self-confidence. Lack of self-confidence is fear, distrust and suspicion, and these things are very bad for our health. In order to become a more sensible person, one must not necessarily follow religious tradition. Without religion one can be a very nice person, a very sensible person. So therefore, wherever I go, I will always talk about the importance of secular ethics.

I think in this country, basically the people are comparatively more religious-minded. But their practice of religion is in the morning, in front of the Ganesh statue or the Shiva lingam, where they close their eyes and recite some Sanskrit shloka without knowing its meaning, then put some flower or incense there. There is no connection to their daily life. So whenever they find the opportunity, corruption happens. These religious people are still corrupted.

So what's lacking? Genuine conviction. You not only need to pray but have conviction as a human being. In order to gain a personal sort of happiness—family happiness, community happiness—the need is to be honest and truthful. This is the key factor that brings inner strength. When you conduct yourself as a truthful and honest person, you can carry on transparently. That brings trust. Trust brings unity and friendship. After all, we are social animals. Cooperation is very essential, now not only on a nation-to-nation basis but also continent-to-continent. Cooperation is really essential and comes on the basis of friendship. With friendship comes trust. Trust comes from compassion. So therefore, these are not only just religious matters, but very important in our day-to-day life. So that I usually try.

So, that's all, thank you.

3

SECULAR ETHICS, HUMAN VALUES AND SOCIETY

Los Angeles, 2011

I thank the organizers for the opportunity to speak and share with people, especially with the youth. I thank myself, too, especially my body. A few days, back I had some throat problems for which I took some medicine, but accidentally I took an overdose and it became a bigger problem. I had a ten-hour sleep at night and I feel very fit today.

I talk about human values wherever I go, as I believe that it is the basis for mental peace and a happy life. No matter what the circumstance, if one is mentally calm, problems can be countered with understanding and ease. They won't be much disturbed mentally, as they are emotionally calm, too. Whether one is a believer or a nonbeliever, there are some very important activities for day-to-day life, like sleeping, which help in improving mental health. Peace of mind is also essential for a healthy mental state; a calm mind and happiness are immensely beneficial to health, too. I am quite sure that if I am not mentally calm then I wouldn't have gotten ten hours of sleep.

You enjoy freedom of community and nation, but by the age of sixteen years, I had lost my freedom, and by the age of twenty-four years, I lost my country. For the last fifty years, I have received occasional good news but most of the time I have received bad news. Despite all that, I strive to keep my mental state very calm. Many people complain a lot about petty issues due to a lack of inner strength. I have always said that in order to be a happy human being, money, fame, power, and a strong body are important, but one should depend on inner strength. Anger does not provide inner strength, even though it temporarily gives a special energy or boldness—but not for long. Therefore, I always promote the importance of inner values. We all are the same human being mentally, physically, and emotionally, and we all want to lead a happy life.

I am a Buddhist, but I believe that harmony between different religions is very important. Some communities, like the Christians or Muslims, have conflict within themselves due to little differences. Conflict between religions is a huge part of human history. All religions may differ, but they have the same core message to impart—to spread and practice compassion, love, forgiveness, and self-discipline. Therefore, there is absolutely no use in creating conflict between different traditions or religions. Holistically, we need different traditions as a variety of mental dispositions needs a variety of traditions to exist. So, the other concept I promote is the concept of harmony between different traditions.

Our first aim is to create a happy world, which is based on a happy community, which in turn is based on a happy family and a happy individual. So, without the happy individual, a happy world cannot be created. Of course, I am a Buddhist and fasting and praying is a part of my life. But one cannot achieve a happy world through prayers. Prayer brings limited benefit to the individual, but none to the world. For a happy world, an individual should be a sensible person and spread the happiness within the family, the community, and then on a national and a global level.

A happy human being does not have to be religious, but should include meditation in his daily life to become a sensible human being. Global level peace cannot be attained through religion because of the existence of a large number of nonbelievers. The main aim is to find a secular way of attaining peace, without touching religion. In the West, my friends who are Christians and Muslims believe that secularism is about disrespecting their religion. But in India, secularism is about respecting all religions and does not give any preference to any religion.

According to my Indian friend, the former deputy prime minister of India, secularism gives respect to nonbelievers too. For more than two thousand years, a small section of philosophers have denied the existence of the next life or the concept of karma. He told me that the section of believers had to face criticism for that view, but they were not disrespected in any manner. So, when I say secular, I don't mean any disrespect to any religion. I am a Buddhist and I believe in religion, but I respect all religions and talk about secularism. With my limited understanding and vocabulary in English, I will try to explain the meaning of secular ethics.

According to me, value means something useful and helpful for our existence. We have a body and a mind, but we need to have a healthy body and a healthy mind. A healthy mind is a phenomenon which involves a subjective way of viewing things. The world of the mind is made of neurons but has different levels, according to Indian psychology. The more subtle-level emotions are based on the sensorial level of the mind; whereas the dream state is the deeper level of mind which does not depend on senses, but depends on five kinds of mental objects.

Dreams, which are the other level of consciousness, are based on experiences or perceptions. Further, the brain function seeks subtle level of consciousness. Some people in India believe that after death, brain function stops but body remains fresh. Scientifically speaking, there are no explanations. But now some research is being conducted regarding this issue. Consciousness of mind in some area has become the subject of discussion. Mind can only have subjective experience which does not have any color or form, but one can only feel. That energy which accompanies the mental process within the technology of reality is part of mantra, not the mind.

In order to achieve a happy life, we need to take care of the body and mind both. Physically, one may be fit but may not be happy. If one takes tranquilizers or alcohol as a medicine for stress then they would feel like animals and will not be able to use human intelligence. The potential of our mind has to be utilized to make sure that education does not go waste. Even though animals have stronger senses than humans as their survival depends on it, we have brains and our thinking power is much more. It is wise to utilize our unique quality in order to attain a calm mind.

The main element, which is needed by people, is warm-heartedness. The mind is divided in two categories—the first is the cognitive level, based on intelligence and emotions, which are linked to motivations. Modern education seems to pay more attention to intelligence and not enough to emotions. Religion emphasizes the development of the other side, the one which is dependent on motivations. Indian tradition has a concept which combines both the categories of mind. The Pope has also emphasized that faith and reason should go together.

Intelligence alone creates more vision, desire and ambition but also brings more fear, suspicion, and distrust. Thus, a balance has to be struck between both the sides of the mind by motivating the emotional side of the mind through warm-heartedness, which will dispel any feeling of distrust. As social animals, humans need an open heart to become a happy individual, family, and community. Within the family, even a little distrust brings fear and loneliness. The emotional experience with the help of intelligence can help a person become happy. If faced with a tragic situation, a person with a balanced mind will be able to overcome the tragic situation easily.

Animals have limited intelligence, so they can't develop good qualities. Humans can inculcate emotions like compassion and warm-heartedness. One form of compassion is biological, which is biased, but the other form of compassion can be cultivated. The cultivated compassion is oriented toward others. Through training, the cherished feeling, compassion for others, forgiveness and genuine concern, with the help of intelligence, can be given to all.

QUESTIONS

QUESTION: *You emphasize compassion as the basis for ethics. But in some situations, isn't ensuring justice necessary, rather than being compassionate to the perpetrator of crime? The death of Osama bin Laden was widely covered by the media, where giving justice to the perpetrator of crime and the news was celebrated by the people. Where does compassion and ethics fit in with that?*

HIS HOLINESS: One should have a clear distinction between the actor and the action. The actions of Osama bin Laden were very destructive. The 9/11 event resulted in the deaths of thousands of people. Justice is needed. But the actor was a human being and we need compassion to deal with him. Steps should be taken to stop the source of destructive action, but the actor can be forgiven. The basis of forgiveness is not forgetting what happened, but remembering what they have done and needing to forgive for mental peace. But serious action needs to have countermeasures to deal with it.

QUESTION: *Religion is the best source of ethics. But sometimes it conflicts with civil law. What should take precedence and why?*

HIS HOLINESS: That depends on the person entirely. If one is a serious believer in religion, then religion becomes important; but if he is a nonbeliever, then the law takes precedence. India has many traditions but is a secular society. India, thus, becomes an example or model for secularism.

In Jodhpur, when I was passing through the hotel lobby, a European man approached me. He had come from Romania to research India's religious harmony. He found a Muslim village with three Hindu families, but there was no fear or conflict, which surprised him. In Kerala, Christians, Muslims, Hindus, and Jains stay together. The relationships are healthy among the people because of secularism, even with the existence of corruption.

For the last fifty-two years, India has been my residence where I feel very safe. Even I should not develop attachment with Buddhism as a biased mind cannot see reality. Any religious follower with too much attachment with their religion, it makes them fanatic, which is a mistake.

QUESTION: *I work in a big corporation and have seen a lot of corruption. If I report it, I will lose my job, and I am the sole breadwinner for my family. What responsibility do I owe to my family and community?*

HIS HOLINESS: It is clearly a sign of corruption. Once when I was in Bombay, a businessman told me that in society there are many corrupted cases and if one is honest then one can't survive. Once a student in Jodhpur told me that an individual can't succeed if he does not take part in some form of corruption. In response to both the cases, I said the majority of the human population has compassion, and it's only some part of the population who are corrupt. One participates in corruption only due to hopelessness. It is a crime and should not go unchecked. It is our duty to raise our voices against it, to stand firm to oppose the spread of such a crime. Some people may get injured in their fight against corruption, but it will be a very a small price to pay for the greater good.

Corrupt people are hypocrites, as they are only concerned about their reputation and work to protect it even when they are aware that what they do is wrong. It's better to live honestly than in hypocrisy. Poor families living with trust are happier than those families who are rich but with very little trust between themselves. The modern education system imparts the importance of material value and not ethics. It is important to build a healthy society through education but not through religion.

QUESTION: *I am soon to finish college and wish my life to be one of service and value. At the same time, many of the opportunities at the corporations don't share my ethics or values. While I think it will be great to work for a non-profit organization or in service of others, necessity is such that I make money in order to pay for my rent and pay off my student loan. Do you have any advice?*

HIS HOLINESS: I will recite Buddha's teaching as the answer—you are the master of your own life. I think you should judge with wider perspective, long-term planning, and honesty. If I advise you something and you face some problem afterward, then you will blame me.

QUESTION: *There are many who are suffering due to the direct consequences of their action. Do you think we have an ethical responsibility to treat them with compassion?*

HIS HOLINESS: The answer will differ according to different philosophical views. For example, according to theistic point of view, everything is God's creation but according to non-theistic religions, like Jainism, Buddhism, and Hinduism, a person has many lives. They believe that some experiences of this lifetime are consequences of their actions in their former life. Thus, it becomes very complicated to address the question.

I believe that everyone should pay more attention to human values and mental awareness. It helps a person's ability to face challenges. So the best advice I can give, and I quote an Indian Buddhist master of the eighth century that if there is a solution, don't be overwhelmed and seek the solution. If there is no solution, then there is no need to be overwhelmed. I agree with this particular teaching because worry just adds up to the stress for the person.

For example, when I visited Japan after the tsunami, I saw the country and remembered a Tibetan saying that described the situation there very aptly—piling of tragedy over tragedy. Catastrophes like the earthquake, tsunami and atomic leak hit Japan one after the other. I told the people that the tragedy is already over, thus no one should worry about it now. All that they can do is work, look forward to the future, and take care of their families. According to the Buddhist point of view, all this is karma. They are passing through a difficult period, but it can be overcome with work and confidence.

QUESTION: *You are the Dalai Lama. Yet you are also human. Have you ever acted unethically?*

HIS HOLINESS: I have often told people that my relationship with the mosquito is not ethical. If there is a danger of malaria, then I act aggressively with them. But if I am in a good mood and there is no danger of malaria, then I am very generous to the mosquito and let it suck my blood. Once I saw that when the mosquito was full of my blood, it just flew away without showing any appreciation. I really think it was a female mosquito as females are more aggressive mosquitoes. It made me curious and once, during a meeting at Oxford University, where I was sitting in front of the dignified professors, I asked them if anyone had an idea about the level of brain size which has the ability to show appreciation. Dogs and cats are capable of showing appreciation. Therefore, on the basis of my observation, I am generous to the first mosquito which sits on me but lose patience with the second, third, or fourth one.

HAMPTON ROADS PUBLISHING COMPANY

. . . for the evolving human spirit

Hampton Roads Publishing Company publishes books on a
variety of subjects, including spirituality, health, and
other related topics.

For a copy of our latest trade catalog, call (978) 465-0504
or visit our distributor's website at *www.redwheelweiser.com*.
You can also sign up for our newsletter and special offers by
going to www.redwheelweiser.com/newsletter/